Outlines of Romantic Theology

OUTLINES OF ROMANTIC THEOLOGY

with which is reprinted

Religion and Love in Dante:
The Theology of Romantic Love

by Charles Williams

Edited and introduced by
ALICE MARY HADFIELD

the apocryphile press
BERKELEY, CA
www.apocryphile.org

apocryphile press
BERKELEY, CA

Apocryphile Press
1700 Shattuck Ave #81
Berkeley, CA 94709
www.apocryphile.org

FirstApocryphile edition, 2005.
For sale in the USA only.
Sales prohibited in the UK.
Printed in the United States of America.

ISBN 0-9764025-8-0

Contents

Editor's Acknowledgments

My principal acknowledgment goes, of course, to that early friend of Charles Williams, the late John Pellow, who lent me his typescript of *Outlines of Romantic Theology* and allowed me to copy it. Short extracts from his diary have been made available to me by Mr. David Dodds, who is carrying out extensive research upon Charles Williams, and by the diary's owner, Dr. R. J. W. Pellow. I am also greatly indebted to Dr. Lyle Dorsett, curator of the Marion E. Wade Collection at Wheaton College, Illinois, who kindly had the original pencilled version of the text copied for me.

I have throughout been greatly encouraged by Mr. Bruce Hunter of David Higham Associates of London, agents for Mr. Michael Williams, owner of the Williams copyrights.

Generous help has also been given me by many members of the Charles Williams Society (c/o The Royal Bank of Scotland, Holt's Branch, Whitehall, London S.W.1, England), especially Dr. Brian Horne, Mr. Martin Moynihan, Dr. Barbara Reynolds, Mrs. Anne Ridler, Mrs. Thelma Shuttleworth, and Mrs. Joan and Mr. Richard Wallis, and also by Mrs. Gillian Stone of Oxford.

Mrs. Susan Cadwallader, my secretary, has been as patient with my disability as she has been efficient with my work. Finally, my husband Charles, who himself once worked with Charles Williams and who later has shared with me a personal exploration of romantic theology, has kindly helped me prepare this book at a time when I had an eyesight problem.

Alice M. Hadfield

Introduction: The Writing of "Outlines of Romantic Theology"

Alice M. Hadfield

Charles Williams was born in London on 20 September 1886 of deeply religious lower-middle-class parents. A sister, Edith, followed him. Charles' quick mind was encouraged by his book-loving father, and when the family moved to St. Albans, a small city twenty miles north of London, Charles was accepted by the best school and did well there.[1]

In 1908 Charles began work at the London office of the Oxford University Press. He was twenty-two and a convinced member of the Anglican Church. Soon afterwards, at a children's party, he met Florence Conway, a dark, good-looking, intelligent teacher. The result was volcanic.

It was perhaps a year later, on a cold January night, that Charles handed Florence the sequence of eighty-four sonnets that was later to be published as *The Silver Stair*.[2] Sonnet 38 is entitled, "That We Know Not Yet What It Is Indeed To Love," and begins:

> I love her. O! what other word could keep
>   In many tongues one clear immutable sound,
>   Having so many meanings? It is bound,
> First, to religion, signifying: "The steep
> Whence I see God," translated into sleep
>   It is: "Glad waking," into thought: "Fixed ground;

1. For a fuller account of Williams's life, see my book *Charles Williams: An Exploration of His Life and Work* (New York: Oxford University Press, 1983).
2. *The Silver Stair* was published in 1912 by Herbert & Daniel.

A measuring-rod," and for the body: "Found."
These know I, with one more, which is: "To weep."

When the sonnets were published in 1912, the Professor of Poetry at Oxford University commented that their author wrote as if he had not suspected there was such a thing as love, and "almost before any touch of familiarity had fallen upon it." Charles had indeed never loved before. Now he felt that he stood on the edge of all possibilities, ready to find out the truth about love for himself and follow where it led. He prefaced the printed book with a quotation from William Butler Yeats' *The Shadowy Waters*:

> It is love that I am seeking for,
> But of a beautiful, unheard-of kind
> That is not in the world.

So began what was to grow into a life-long study, the working out, through his own experience and that of the poets, of a theory of romantic theology.

He meant, I think, by "romance" what John Buchan once called "strangeness flowering from the commonplace," or, if you like, making the ordinary extraordinary. For sex, love, and marriage are commonplace and ordinary; they can also and at the same time be strange and extraordinary. Romance, he felt, does not stand by itself; it is an aspect of the multiform relationship of men, women, and God, the study of which is theology's business. Romantic theology is, therefore, the working out of ways in which an ordinary relationship between two people can become one that is extraordinary, one that grants us glimpses, visions of perfection.

Here it is, in his own words, written in pre-marriage days:

> Where did you meet your love, young man?
> Where did you meet your love?
> 'I met my love in a noisy room
> With a carven roof above.'
>
> What did you say to your love, young man,
> With all your mother wit?
> ' "How hot it is!" or "How do you do?"
> And there was an end of it!'

Who was beside you then, young man?
Who was beside you then?
'Gaspar, Melchior, Balthazar,
And a crowd of shepherd-men!'

What did you say to them, young man,
Silently, through the din?
' "Princes, when ye come in to her,
I pray you, lead me in." '

"In the Land of Juda," in *Poems of Conformity*, 1917

He and Florence were married quietly in 1917 in St. Albans Abbey. He had thought nervously of this necessary step, but he took it, moving into a second stage of development—love in marriage and fatherhood. Three volumes of poetry followed: *Poems of Conformity* (1917), *Divorce* (1920),[3] and *Windows of Night* (early 1925, but written earlier). All three were published by Humphrey Milford, head of the Oxford University Press's London branch.

Two influences may have suggested a book on romantic love: Dante and Malory's *Morte d'Arthur.* Charles Williams discovered Dante, both in *The New Life* and in *The Divine Comedy,* and thus found another soul upon whom love had wrought powerfully; he had also since his youth been concerned with finding new meanings and insights within the Arthurian stories told by Malory. Yet the efficient cause of his writing *Outlines of Romantic Theology* may well have been Coventry Patmore, the religiously-minded and enthusiastic Victorian poet of married love. Williams's own marriage, the insights he had been trying to work out in his volumes of poetry, and the stimulus of the Oxford University Press's move in 1924 to beautiful, spacious offices in eighteenth-century Amen House, formed the background. Could the idea of writing down what he had discovered have come from the Prologue to Patmore's *The Angel in the House?*

The poet, looking for a theme "in green and undiscover'd ground," tells his wife

3. The title refers to the death of his father and their consequent separation, not to his marriage.

INTRODUCTION

> "I have the very well-head found
> Whence gushes the Pierian Spring."

She asks what the subject is to be,

> "The Life
> Of Arthur, or Jerusalem's Fall?"

and is told

> "Neither: your gentle self, my Wife,
> And love, that grows from one to all."

Indeed Williams could well have chosen Arthur, as he did later in other books, though he never followed Tasso to Jerusalem. Instead, like Patmore, he began to write down what he had discovered about love and marriage. So, probably in a few weeks, he wrote *Outlines of Romantic Theology*, his first prose book—he himself describes it as a pamphlet.

His friend John Pellow—a learned and lively fellow poet—wrote of Williams in his diary on 21 August 1924: "he is writing *Outlines of Romantic Theology*, a prose version of *Divorce*, and *Conformity*..." Pellow had not, of course, then seen *Windows of Night*, which was to be published a few months later.

I have chosen a quotation from each book to illustrate Pellow's remark:

> Hands, bound but to a simple pledge,
> Discover new vocation;
> Instincts, our bodies' depths that dredge,
> Grow teachers of salvation.
>
> O who can doubt the perfect Whole
> In his eternal trysting,—
> Love, of the reasonable soul
> And human flesh subsisting!
>
> From "Commentaries V," in *Poems of Conformity*

> Then surging from those portals the mind of Wordsworth drew
> Immortal strength from woods and hills, and undefeated flew

The Burning Heart of Dante, and all of matter strove
To aid the arms of Mansoul[4] in nature and in love.

From "Ballad of Material Things," in *Divorce*

Once in a glory
To my heart he came,
Born of a maiden,
With love for his name;
But what bitter passion
On myself for tree
Hath his bounty suffered!
Now deep in me,
Silent, unmanifest,
Hiding his power,
During a time and times,
Waits he his hour.

From "Saint Mary Magdalene," in *Windows of Night*

The prefatory quotation to *Outlines of Romantic Theology*, "Have I been so long with you, and yet hast thou not known me, Philip?" (John 14:9), gives us a clue to its theme. In experiencing romantic love, we experience God: He has been in the experience from the beginning, and the more we learn about it, the more we learn also about Him. Charles writes as a Christian and his book is firmly placed within the Christian tradition, but it need not be; for is not some experience of the supernatural part of any deeply-felt love, especially one that leads to marriage and family?

The book, I think, is Charles stating his position. Perhaps he felt obscurely that his love for, and marriage to, Florence was not widening and deepening as it should. He was quite right. Maybe he was, to use his own phrase, keeping back "something of the price" (see p. 51); maybe Florence was over-concentrating on their one child and under-participating in Charles' quickly opening life at the Press. Be that as it may, turmoil lay close ahead.

The stages of the book's writing are difficult to understand. I think

4. The city of Mansoul, the soul of man, in John Bunyan's allegory *The Holy War*.

that it was written in longhand early in 1924, and then typed, probably by his sister Edith. In that form it was shown to his friend John Pellow, and probably also to those whose initials are given in the dedication. I have a copy of Pellow's comments and Williams's notes upon them, which refer to page numbers that run continuously and suggest a finished text rather shorter than we now have. He was probably pulling together such comments from his friends when he wrote wryly to Pellow on 5 September 1924: "I scribble away at *Romantic Theology*, a book which will probably affect profoundly the whole thought of the Universal Church."

This same typescript must have been submitted to Humphrey Milford at about the same time that Williams sent it to his friends, for on 6 September he writes again to Pellow: "T. B. Ripon has reported but secretly—at least, Caesar[5] hides the document: which infuriates me. I have hinted at openness, without effect. Caesar, in a private note to me, says (most charmingly): 'I fear this is not for us. It may be for all time and I may be like the poor Indian,[6] but I am afraid of it and of you.' So the unfortunate *Romantic Theology* shall cuddle the equally unfortunate *Chapel of the Thorn*[7] in a private seclusion. . . . Well, actually they shall be in a public seclusion—since whoever wants to read them may." If "T. B. Ripon" stands for "The Bishop of Ripon," it seems that Milford asked him for a report on Williams's typescript, after which Milford wrote his note to Williams.

With my own publishing background, I find it very odd that Williams did not wait to submit a finished manuscript to such a key

---

5. "Caesar"= Humphrey Milford.

6. In "the poor Indian" I think Milford mixed two well-known quotations:

> Lo! the poor Indian, whose untutored mind
> Sees God in clouds, or hears him in the wind.

(Pope, *An Essay on Man*, Epistle I, lines 99-100)

> one whose hand,
> Like the base Indian, threw a pearl away
> Richer than all his tribe.

(Shakespeare, *Othello*, act 5, scene 2, lines 345-47)

7. An early verse play, of which only a few stanzas are known to survive.

figure as his own employer, so that he in turn could have sent it to an outside reader. It is even odder, perhaps, that Williams could expect to see such a reader's report, which in my experience would always be treated as at any rate partly confidential.

However, he continued to write. On 16 September 1924 he wrote Pellow, thanking him for some theological references and saying: "The book, with several lacunae, is now finished. But the lacunae will take some filling up." Oddly, at this point he seems to have rewritten the whole book in longhand, in pencil, on small sheets about eight inches by five inches in size, adding several new paragraphs while doing so. This manuscript survives in the Marion E. Wade Collection at Wheaton College, Illinois.

On October 3 he told Pellow that "*Romantic Theology* is temporarily finished, but it is only in pencil and I don't know when I shall have it typed. However, it shall be yours when I do." It was indeed re-typed, probably again by his sister, for by June 1925 a colleague, Fred Page, had sent it to the Nonesuch Press, by whom it was rejected. Pellow then asked Williams to be allowed to borrow it, and he noted in his diary on June 22: "A rare and wonderful book (I read the first 2 or 3 chapters in the evening)." At the end of that year Osbert Burdett—reader to the new firm of Faber & Gwyer (now Faber & Faber)—was shown a copy. He liked it, told Pellow that it was "beautifully written," and recommended it, though he asked Williams to consider lengthening it if he could do so without spoiling it, to change the title, and to consider having a preface. Pellow tells us that Williams was "violently indignant" with these suggestions, "but it didn't mean much," and that he adopted "with enthusiasm" Pellow's suggested title, *Intelletto d'Amore: An Introduction to Romantic Theology*. Nevertheless, Faber & Gwyer delayed a decision, for it was the year of Britain's General Strike and the economic outlook was uncertain, and finally asked Williams to resubmit it the following year. He did not do so, and seems to have lost interest in it, perhaps because so much in his private life had changed since it had been written.

Only one typed copy is known, that owned by the late John Pellow, who many years ago allowed me to take a photocopy. This is used for the present text. The omission of the promised quotations in the first chapter (see p. 10) and the fact that many other quotations in the text are clearly written from memory and are not completely accurate at first suggested to me that a final version, now lost, once existed—one shown to the Nonesuch Press and Faber & Gwyer. However, I now incline to the view that, because of loss of interest, no such version was ever prepared.

A few minor spelling mistakes or errors of punctuation in the typescript have been corrected without comment; all other discrepancies have been noted.

OUTLINES OF ROMANTIC THEOLOGY

"Have I been so long with you, and yet hast thou not known me, Philip?" [1]

1. John 14:9.

To A. H. E. L., D. H. S. N., and F. P.,[2]
whose book this is as much or more than mine

2. The initials are those of the Reverend Henry Lee, Daniel Nicholson
Frederick Page. For information about these three friends, the last-named a
colleague at the Oxford University Press, see the index to my book *Charles William
Exploration of His Life and Work* (New York: Oxford University Press, 1983).

Contents

CHAPTER I

The Term "Romantic Theology"

Theology, which is the science of God, is generally divided into various classes: Dogmatic, Moral, Pastoral, Ascetic, Mystical. But there is a side of it which is concerned with so definite an experience and such exact intellectual deductions that it may be convenient to regard it as a class in itself; more especially as it has, on the whole, been rather neglected by experts in the other divisions, and left to the poets and artists. The name given to this side of the science might well be Romantic Theology. This term does not imply, as will inevitably at first be thought, a theology based merely on fantasy and dream, and concerning itself only with illogical sentimentalities. It is a theology as exact as any other kind, but having for cause and subject those experiences of man which, anyhow in discussions of art, are generally termed "Romantic". The chief of these is romantic love; that is, sexual love between a man and a woman, freely given, freely accepted, and appearing to its partakers one of the most important experiences in life—a love which demands the attention of the intellect and the spirit for its understanding and its service. That there are other human experiences of this same far-reaching nature is undeniable—nature and friendship are perhaps the chief, and these will be touched on in the last section of this essay. But this book is concerned almost entirely to make some attempt to formulate, for the help of students, the principles of Romantic Theology as applicable to romantic love; and it does not profess to do more than sketch the outlines of the subject. The excuse for its existence is that, though a good deal has been written on the subject, especially by the great love poets, the author does not know of any book which attempts to make

7

a beginning of it as a scientific theological study. That a similar formulation may exist, somewhere in the vast mass of Christian theology, is only too probable, but if so, it does not appear to be particularly well-known at the present day, and the present essay may therefore fall into the hands of some student of the subject who is, like the author, unacquainted with its predecessor. To students who do not accept the doctrine of the Incarnation, the suggestions made will probably appear fanciful; it is at any rate certain, as a compensation, that to no Christian can they appear as anything but natural and probable, even if in the end they should have to be, for one cause or another, rejected. In a sense, of course, any such study as the present is negligible, as all intellectual formulation of spiritual experience, and all schematization of it, is negligible. There are lovers, as there are saints, in all ages, who not only do not know but do not care to know, anything of the work of the mind, and they are sometimes the greatest lovers and saints. No knowledge of Dogmatic Theology is a substitute for a saving faith; nor of Moral Theology for the formation of the habit of moral obedience; nor of Mystical Theology for the practice of communion with God. Nor is any theoretical doctrine in Romantic Theology the satisfactory equivalent for its practice. But theory may be a help to practise, and even sometimes an incentive to it. Romantic Theology is no more than a basis, but the possibility of its sometimes being that is a reason for its formulation.

Since Romantic Theology is a part of Christian Theology it will be understood that this essay is written entirely from the point of view of an orthodox Christian. The Rites and dogmas of Christianity, as set forth in the *Book of Common Prayer* of the Church of England, are assumed on the one side, as romantic love is assumed on the other. Intellectually, such a position implicitly assumes that the theologies of other religions are mistaken, but it is not, of course, denied that romantic lovers in any part or any age of the world have achieved their proper end under whatever creed they professed. The present business is merely the formulation of Christian theology; not a denial or correction of others.

But if this side of the book is limited, the other is universal. Love, as previously defined, is a normal human thing, although its development and progress must be modified and defined by the particular habits, social and religious, of its environment. It is, in another sense

than that of the Vincentian canon, held *semper et ubique et ab omnibus.*[1]
It has been part of the work of Christianity in the world to make men
aware of the spiritual significance of certain natural experiences. This
has been attempted with sacrifice, it has been attempted with death; it
has been attempted very little with romantic love. Yet any human energy
that can be so described is capable of being assumed into sacramental
and transcendental heights—such is the teaching of the Incarnation.
Thus the distance between an ordinary meal and that nourishment
which is communicated in the Eucharist should lessen, as it were, until
perhaps to the devout soul every meal is an actual Eucharist in the
theological sense. Nor would such a progress involve any invasion of
the order of the Church, for it would be an additional and free grace of
God. But much theology has been spent upon this sacrament, whereas
comparatively little has been written upon the other sacrament of
marriage. In general, the Church has confined herself to exhorting the
newly married pair to observe their moral duties and their ecclesiastical,
and to repudiating divorce more or less strenuously. And yet the
universality, the intensity, and (one might almost say) the necessity of
love, might have suggested it as a subject for the most profound
consideration. Such consideration the Church may yet find it possible
to give, and that will be the Age of Romantic Theology. It has been
prevented from doing so in the past by various causes. For example,
during the earliest age of the Church her expectation of the immediate
return of Christ distracted her mind from a subject which implied
children and the continuance of the world. Again, her inevitable
concentration upon another world, her existence, so to speak, in that
world and merely partial appearance in this, tends to cause her to
neglect the affairs of this world; and by consequence to regard with
suspicion any sacrament accompanied by and indeed consisting of
human delight. The Church has always, not unnaturally, been haunted
by a Manicheanism which, driven out by dogma, has returned as a
vaguer but pervading influence. This added to that necessary asceticism
which is the prelude to the profounder depths of mystical life has

---

1. A shortened version of St. Vincent of Lerins' "Quod semper, quod ubique,
quod ab omnibus creditum est" ("What is always, what is everywhere, what is by all
people believed").

resulted in an attitude towards marriage that seems to regard it, though officially calling it a sacrament, as in effect nothing much more than a matter of morals. Probably this attitude has been strengthened by the celibacy of the clergy, so long and so widely maintained. It would be demanding too much of the theologians, for most of them have been clerics, to expect them to be sensitive to the meaning and graces of a sacrament from which they have been debarred. In this only of the sacraments are the priesthood not merely unessential in times of necessity, but almost unimportant at any time. Compelled by the Mind of the Church to perform the ecclesiastical ceremony of marriage whenever it is demanded, they find the same Mind declaring that the celebrants of the sacrament are, always and everywhere, the two lovers; that the ecclesiastical ceremony, though of the *bene esse,* is not of the *esse,* of it; and that in consequence the priest, though a witness terrestrial and celestial, whose presence it would be the highest insolence not to invite, is hardly more. The position is novel, and the result not amazing.

That the result, the neglect by theology of marriage as a sacrament, is undoubted could be shown by many quotations.[2]

These then are the official utterances, or rather the utterances of the officials of the Church, which is not quite the same thing. They are concerned largely with such moral matters as divorce and birth-control and so forth, a side of the subject with which this essay does not concern itself (except incidentally, so far as divorce is concerned, in a few tentative suggestions). And yet something may be gathered from the attitude which the Church has taken up on those matters, little as its officials (with few and lovely exceptions) seem to understand it. To them in some way divorce and birth-control seem to have existed in no relation to marriage: awful laws of the Absolute. It is the old error of substituting the very proper negation of certain means for the assertion of the end which is to be attained, *not* by those means. In marriage, as everywhere else, the Church is concerned with the regeneration of man. This regeneration, which will probably take aeons before it can be dimly

---

2. After this paragraph Williams clearly intended to add a number of quotations, as is shown by the words that follow. In the MS Williams notes an intended quotation from a Vatican council and comments upon it. The passage is then deleted, and the typist is told to begin a fresh page.

foreseen, is not to be brought about by an evasion of the problem. Now divorce and birth-control are both, in effect, evasions of the problem. It is the man and the marriage that is the problem. If you dissolve the marriage, if you artificially dissolve the connexion between intercourse and birth, you may (with the happiest temporal results) evade the problem, but you have not solved it. It is, on the part of the Church, an instinctive grasp of this fact that has made her cling almost with passion to the problem; and has made her look such an obstinate fool to everyone else. She may, in a sense, fail to solve the problem; humanly speaking, she has often failed, but she will not deny or evade it. There is no solution except some sort of regeneration, of transmutation, what you will; and the awful eyes that are fixed on eternity see this, though the "No, no, no" of her outcry sounds more like the voice of a peevish child or an hysterical woman.*

Such is the present ecclesiastical position. But its unsatisfactory nature is accentuated by the present secular position; chiefly, by the flood of sex literature which has drowned the modern world. Our poetry, our fiction, our drama, our journalism, are full of it, from Shakespeare and Marlowe (who invented it) to the middle page of any morning paper. It may be rightly argued that with great literature, say *Antony and Cleopatra*, one is concerned with poetry and not with sex. But though this is true of it all separately from *Tamburlaine* to *The Ring and the Book* or *Emblems of Love*,[3] it remains also true that the continual choice of romantic love as a subject has the effect of constantly directing the attention of the mind to romantic love: a constancy of attention which is very bad for an unprincipled mind, and not too good for a principled.

---

* Mr. D. H. S. Nicholson, in an admirable skit, has presented a land where everyone grows enormously fat on a very ordinary diet, and where the Church vigorously opposes the general introduction of a medicine after taking which meals can be freely eaten without any fear of too much fat. It is to be feared that the Church would do so. It is also credible that the Church would be right. Medicine in such a case would again evade the problem, though alas, how beautifully! [Textual note by Williams]

[For D. H. S. Nicholson, see my note on the book's dedication on page 3.—ED. NOTE]

3. *Tamburlaine the Great*, a blank verse play (written not later than 1587) by Christopher Marlowe (1564–1593); *The Ring and the Book*, a poem (published in 1868 and 1869) by Robert Browning (1812–1889); *Emblems of Love*, a book of dramatic poems (published 1912) by Lascelles Abercrombie (1881–1938).

11

Nor has this concentration of literature upon it been any too good for romantic love itself. There is in love, as in religion, a hypocrisy, or at any rate a foolish optimism, which is exceedingly like the truth but is not the truth. It is no doubt true, as the Lady Julian of Norwich saw, that in the providence of God, all things are well even at this present moment, "all things are most well";[4] but this is very different from a well-to-do tradesman's assurance that everything's for the best. So in love it is most certain that the lovers are manifest to each other's eyes in their original perfection; but this is not the same thing as the rather silly convention of romance that only a pretended criticism of the beloved should be allowed a place. The romantic mind must, if it is to be justified, work within the bounds of realism; as indeed love itself does, for of all proverbs that which declares that "Love is blind" is surely the most foolish. Love can only see the next world by virtue of that eyesight which sees and is not afraid to see the flaws in this; all other vision is blindness, all other faith superstition.

That it can go on, this mush of sentimentality, this glowing romance, is to be doubted. Three things can happen—perhaps one, perhaps all, will. First, there may be a reaction; we may pass off on to some other subject. It is to be hoped we shall. Second, we may proceed, with Mr. D. H. Lawrence, over the edge of humanity, into some very real but rather awful physical mysticism, a mysticism already adumbrated by Rossetti and Swinburne. Thirdly, Theology may take the marsh in hand and try to drain it. In such a work this book tries, perhaps vainly, to handle a spade. But it does so, not with any wish to sentimentalise still further an over-sentimentalised age; but with the hope of canalising our emotions, leaving the rest of the land dry for purposes of cultivation of other crops, and establishing a means of transport by which such vessels as choose may proceed more effectively to their end.

For convenience' sake, and in order to avoid too much talk about love, the word "marriage" is used to cover the whole process of love from its first appearance between two people to its remote and indefinable end; the rite of marriage and married life, as ordinarily understood, will be referred to in clear terms when necessity arises. It should also be said that although the discussion throughout tends to be conducted from

4. Lady Julian of Norwich (1342–after 1416) wrote *The Sixteen Revelations of Divine Love,* from which the quoted phrase is taken, in 1393.

the point of view of the man, anything that is postulated of his experiences is postulated also of the woman's. Any differences in the deductions drawn from those rival and correlated experiences will be a matter for students when the principles have been laid down.

CHAPTER II

The Principles

The principles of Romantic Theology can be reduced to a single formula: which is, the identification of love with Jesus Christ, and of marriage with His life. This again may be reduced to a single word—Immanuel. Everything else is modification and illustration of this. Romantic Theology, like the rest, is therefore first of all a Christology.

But certain explanations of this principle may very well be made here, explanations necessitated by Christian dogma. Thus, the identification of love with Jesus Christ is an identification with Him as God as well as Man, but not with absolute Deity. As Christ himself prayed to the Father and is himself included in the entire Trinity, so romantic love does not exalt itself, even at its most mystical, beyond an assumption into Deity. The *Pater Noster*[1] remains, though with certain special applications, a prayer to a greater than it.

Again, this identification does not in any sense set up to be the only identification possible of human love with Christ. As Christ is less than the whole Trinity, so romantic love is less than Christ. It is assumed into Him with the rest of manhood, though in a particular and more obviously symbolical manner. The love of friends, the love of nature, the love of places, are no doubt also one with Him, but they are not our present purpose.

Lastly, this identification—the caution is perhaps unnecessary?—is in no sense brought about by man, any more than the Mass is the result of our efforts. Every Mass was said once on Calvary, and we do

1. The Lord's Prayer. See Matthew 6:9-13.

not so much repeat as are in the Mass absorbed into that eternal offering. So each marriage was lived in His life, though—in terms of time—it waits its due time in the order of the universe to become manifest. Whether they are conscious of it or not, no pair of true lovers are in their history more than this accorded manifestation. Their business is not to be, but to know that they are, His symbols, and that their marriage is His life.

For, subject to the theologians, it may be urged that all the deeds and sayings of Christ are eternal as well as temporal; and that therefore they are universal in their application. Each of them is absorbed into His eternity and thence given out again, with exact application, to every instant of created life. To take an example, each of Christ's denunciations of the priesthood is applicable not only to all priesthood but to that principle in each of us by which we become, each in our place, priests of the Divine Perfection. This and all the applications are not always obvious, but they are assuredly there, and He applies them as they become essential. It is His manifestation of Himself in marriage which is the subject of Romantic Theology.

It was said that marriage is to be identified with His life. The rest of this section will devote itself to certain suggestions of the identification. The emphasis of course varies with each pair of lovers, but the broad facts are the same everywhere, in virtue of that identity of principle, and the details will be understood by each pair separately. To some the Temptation, to some the Ministry, to some the Crucifixion, to some (most happy) the Resurrection, will seem to be the supreme facts. Each to his own experience, but none must deny the others, for the dogmas of the Catholic Church forbid.

We begin then with the Birth and with the Mother of God. And it is with her that the parallel becomes first apparent. It is wiser here to say parallel, for the Blessed Virgin was but one human soul, and is not therefore to be identified with any other, although Christ who is Man is (in the end) to be identified with all. For the exactest statements of the birth of love and the beginning of marriage we have to go to the poets; it is they who have most truly expressed a general experience. It is in its earliest moments rather a delight of contemplation than a desire of union; being its own satisfaction and asking for nothing more. And though this desire is probably necessary, in order that contemplation may become ever more rich and full, the heart is often so shaken by the mere contemplation of the beloved that it is not conscious of anything beyond its own delight. The whole person of the lover is possessed by a new state of consciousness; love is born in him. "They have changed eyes", says Shakespeare.[2] But in this state of love he sees and contemplates the beloved as the perfection of living things: love is bestowed by her smile; she is its source and its mother. She appears to him, as it were, archetypal, the alpha and omega of creation; without father or mother, without human ties of any sort, for she is before humanity, the first-created of God. To her, for example, may be decently applied all the titles of the Litany of Loretto[3] (and it is the business of Romantic Theology to urge and to prove that they may be justly so applied). She is the Mother of Love, purissima, inviolata, admirabilis;[4] she is the Maid, virgo veneranda, potens, clemens;[5] she is the mirror of all mystical titles—speculum iustitiae, sedes sapientiae, causa nostrae laetitiae, domus aurea, stella matutina, salus infirmorum:[6] Unless the identification of marriage love with Christ be accepted, to press the similarity farther would seem profane. But any lover to whom the application of the titles we have quoted seems natural and right may believe from that in the Godhead of Incarnate Love, and may so dare to apply in a very real sense the titles which remain—Mater divinae gratiae, Mater Salvatoris, Rosa mystica, Refugium peccatorum, Regina Prophetarum.[7] Not certainly of herself is she anything but as being glorious in the delight taken in her by the Divine Presence that accompanies her, and yet is born of her; which created her and is helpless as a child in her power. However in all other ways she may be full of error or deliberate

---

2. *The Tempest*, act 1, scene 2, line 444.

3. According to the *Oxford Dictionary of the Christian Church*, the Litany of Loretto is "a Litany in honour of the Blessed Virgin Mary, consisting of a series of invocations of our Lady under various honorific titles, . . . each followed by the request: 'Pray for us'" (2d ed., ed. F. L. Cross and E. A. Livingstone [London: Oxford University Press, 1974], p. 827).

4. Most pure, inviolate, admirable.

5. Venerable, powerful, merciful.

6. Mirror of justice, seat of wisdom, cause of our joy, house of gold, morning star, health of the sick.

7. Mother of divine grace, Mother of our Savior, mystical Rose, refuge of sinners, Queen of Prophets.

evil, in the eyes of the lover, were it but for a moment, she recovers her glory, which is the glory that Love had with the Father before the world was. Immaculate she appears, Theotokos,[8] the Mother of God.

Here then is this supreme woman; here is this supreme experience. Now it is a matter of common note, that this experience does at once, as it were, establish itself as the centre of life. Other activities are judged and ordered in relation to it; they take on a dignity and seem to be worth while because of some dignity and worth which appears to be inherent in life itself—life being the medium by which love is manifested. A lover will regard his own body and its functions as beautiful and hallowed by contact with hers, and indeed it seems often to be in some degree purified by neighbourhood. His intellectual powers will be renewed and quickened in the same way. And—if Romantic Theology is correct—his soul itself will enter upon a new state, becoming conscious of that grace of God which is otherwise, for so many, difficult to appreciate. It does not, therefore, seem indecent to recognise in this centralising of the physical and mental round love the adoration of the Shepherds and the Magi.[9] The animal nature, the most high Imaginations, find here a greater than themselves: "Unto you," said the angel to the Shepherds, "is born this day a Saviour." "We have seen His Star in the East," said the Magians, "and are come to worship Him." It is, to the one as to the other, unexpected. On whatever search the mind—the Imagination, rather; it is the nobler and exacter term; for it is vision, not logic, that is in question—has been engaged, politics or art or life and the nature of the gods, it realises that here is something which it must take into account, not as a mere detail, but as a serious and central thing. Not that this thing itself is of obvious worth: a girl and a delight are no more visibly the centre of the universe than a girl and a baby. But if they argue they argue against a star, as the Magi might have argued against it; and the natural instincts of the lover say, exactly as the Shepherd did, "Come, let us see this thing which is come to pass, which the Lord hath made known to us."

This phrase brings us to the next point in the identification of marriage with the life of Christ. Until this study has been developed further by the Mind of the Church, some of these identifications must

8. God-bearer.
9. See Luke 2:8-20 and Matthew 2:1-12.

17

be tentative. And this particular one—which is, the Presentation in the Temple[10]—will depend very largely upon the degree to which the lover, and the beloved, for it should be a common (if separate and silent) act, deliberately refer themselves to God. It may very well be held that some such reference does, as a matter of fact, take place in the consciousness of every right lover, whatever his intellectual beliefs may be. But at any rate in all orthodox lovers, the first step after their recognition of the fact of love will be its presentation to God. They may not regard love as God, as possibly the Blessed Virgin and Saint Joseph did not understand fully "that holy thing" which they took to the Temple. But that will be for the future to make clear.

A point of discussion for students may be whether Christ in fact identifies this presentation with His own Presentation or with His Baptism.[11] But the Baptism would seem to correspond more closely with the ceremonial marriage; as being a public act preceding a public life, whereas the Presentation in the Temple was private and preceded that retired life of growth in His home which corresponds very naturally to the retired growth of love in the lovers during the period preceding the ceremonial marriage. The two incidents are nevertheless very closely related, and, inasmuch as the ceremonial is only of importance because "it becometh us to fulfil all righteousness"[12] it is not of vast concern. The whole life of love may have been fulfilled before the ceremony takes place, even (though this is probably rare) to the full Resurrection and Ascension.

To return to the main theme. The Presentation in its original act held within it an incident not unimportant to the lover, the prophecy of Simeon.[13] In that prophecy the Blessed Virgin was warned of the sword that should pierce her own heart, the Seven Sorrows which should wound her immaculate tenderness. The lover then who applies this prophecy to himself and to the beloved—for though the beloved is at first more particularly the symbol of Mary, the lover is united with her in that motherhood and is subjected to her destiny—such a lover will hear the great tradition of the Church proclaiming the hour of his dereliction. Indeed such a prophecy may already have stirred in his heart

10. See Luke 2:22-39.
11. See Matthew 3:13-17.
12. Matthew 3:15.
13. Luke 2:25-35.

if—in the early hours of Bethlehem—he regards with fixed attention the history of Christ. It may have stirred also at the preliminary hints of that normal human relapse and boredom which follows swiftly on any high experience, and it is in a sense a relief to him to find his distress at this collapse already in being,—a collapse demanded not by his weakness but by the order of the universe, and to be accepted therefore not so much as a collapse as a part of the mystery of love.

This prophecy which was made of Christ and is to be applied to love is naturally to be connected with such an incident as the Massacre of the Innocents.[14] In this directly love is not involved; his death is not yet. But it remains—perhaps in general, certainly in Romantic, theology—a most significant fact. For it is the destruction by Herod of all the holy instincts of the soul. Herod is Desire establishing itself in the Sacred City—the usurper, the tyrant, the destroyer. It is not the guilt of the lovers that brings about the Massacre which yet fails in its object; the later attempt upon him does not fail, for Judas is not yet of the company of the initiates. It is, so to speak, the immediate pressure of the mad government of the world, a sudden strong assault upon the Holy Thing which threatens the world. The same Herodian house which slays the Innocents slays the Baptist, the greatest of the prophets, the greatest teacher of the lover before love is born in him—Justice or Fortitude or Temperance or any of their servants in literature or life. From this attack Love takes refuge in flight; and it may be that, in the lives of many lovers at any rate, he never returns from that inner exile, or returns only to dwell secretly even from them in some spiritual Nazareth of his choice. "Out of Egypt have I called my son",[15] and Egypt is perhaps the place of formally-accepted marriage. All the Holy Innocents, all the supernatural impulses, are destroyed save only this, and Egypt adores the God with feigned myths and by another name than Immanuel. These Egyptians, conventionally established in married households, hold him as an alien, and by their very conventions bear witness to the truth; as if Mrs. Grundy[16] were a dim shadow of the holy

14. Matthew 2:13-18.
15. Matthew 2:15, referring to Hosea 11:1.
16. Mrs. Grundy: originally a non-appearing character in T. Morton's play *Speed the Plough* (1798); later a symbol of propriety.

and glorious Mother of God. It is perhaps not merely by chance that the greatest thing that Egypt has left to us of another dispensation is the Book of the Dead. But the happier lovers, more fortunate though destined to a deeper agony, return with him, and upon the Nativity and the first shock of contact with the world, the flesh, and the devil, follows the silent growth of Nazareth.

These years of retirement are, in their nature, impossible to discuss; in them the Divine Child increases and thrives in favour with God and Man under the private guardianship of the two lovers. He is subject to them, while at the same time they "keep all these things and ponder them in their hearts".[17] This secret growth is prolonged until the time of the Baptism or its equivalent, which has been already mentioned. It is clear that the Baptism is a ceremony which Love insists on observing, yet a ceremony declared to be unnecessary, and performed by a minister who is less than the subject of the rite. The ceremony of Marriage, according to the Mind of the Church, is to be observed, yet is in itself unnecessary, and the priest performing it is less than the Love which undergoes his blessing.

Upon the ceremonial marriage follows immediately the Temptation.[18] It has been observed often that unlike so many tales of Divine Heroes, the story includes no temptation by women. But is this, which is suitable to the trial of Man, suitable also to the trial of married lovers? Again, in what sense, it may be asked, are lovers (as such) subjected to any such temptations as are recorded? The answer to both questions is the same—to remind ourselves that we are discussing the temptation, not of lovers, but of Love.

This is bound up with and is another example of the whole thesis—that the work of redemption which Christ carried out in his earthly life is manifested and fulfilled in his mystical life of Love. Of that earthly life the Temptation is perhaps one of the most difficult episodes to realize; it is easier to believe that God could suffer through his creatures' deeds than that he could be tempted. But indeed all the three temptations are really but one, to hasten in some way for his own benefit

17. This quotation is adapted from Luke 2:19: "But Mary kept all these things, and pondered them in her heart."
18. See Matthew 4:1-11.

the process which is Himself. The Temptation of Love is to overwhelm the lovers, to hypnotise them as it were, and reduce them, willing or unwilling, to a state of passivity which is actually, in the end, the state they desire. But this slowly attained passivity is to be a state throbbing with deliberate choice, vibrant with the infinite moments of choice by which it is slowly induced. In this sense many lovers would wish only that he would yield to the Temptation, and would compel them to be his slaves and puppets. Who would desire free will if by any means this most awful and bitter of all gifts could be removed from man, especially man in a state of love? But alas, he sustains, he rejects this Temptation; he prefers to that apocalypse, the ministry, the Passion, the Church; and in this choice the lovers have no part. They may indeed have to endure the desert and the fast; but it is because their consciousness is relentlessly driven up there with Christ by the Spirit. It is not they who can convert the stones of depression, boredom, monotony, dislike, into bread: it is He who is tempted to do so and refrains. For if they fast in a desert with Him, they are nevertheless there already; it is their hearts which are the stones at His feet. Doubtless He could change them by a miracle, as doubtless also He could maintain His royalty by the glory of His continual obvious kingdom over them, or by maintaining Himself against all the laws of natural things. But doubtless also, as He chose not to do it then He chooses not to do it now. He awaits the choice of men, the continual choice of the lovers; He will not by any greater miracle than the memory of Bethlehem or the Transfiguration[19] which He deigns to his proved elect on some mountain of their journey compel or persuade their devotion.

Anything that can be said of the three years' ministry can better be said in the next section upon the New Testament. We may pass on to that obscure story of the Passion of Love. For this supreme loss the lovers have been prepared by the Prophecy of Simeon, the Massacre of the Innocents, the fast in the desert, and other hints and warnings. Nevertheless, even after a long experience there are few lovers in whose twelve-fold personality* there is not something akin to Judas and the

---

19. See Matthew 17:1-9.

* This is not the place to enlarge upon it, but obviously, as Christ is the synthesis of the positive, and the Blessed Virgin of the receptive, side of man, so the Twelve are

abyss—something, not heroic or apocalyptic in its superb defiance of good, but mean and small and creeping like theft from a friend's money which is entrusted to the pilferer. It is by the unseen growth of such meannesses that Love comes to his doom; and since that Death is assuredly consummated in a universal and historic sense in Jesus Christ it remains true that even such lovers (if any there be) who are free from all taint of impurity must yet be willing—like mystics of high sanctity— to accept the departure of their All. That this departure in all cases takes place does not follow; that is a matter for Love, and for Love only, to decide according to His needs; but the willingness must be there. The results of such a Death to the lovers need not be enlarged upon; they, like the Mother of God, are commended to some other and much lesser power—morality or courtesy or prophecy or mortal faith in love.

It was noted that the Massacre of the Innocents took place under the rule of Herod, Desire and Possession ruling with power. But the Death of Love seems to demand for its accomplishment, not only Herod, not only Judas, but Caiaphas and Pilate. And Caiaphas *was* the high priest and Pilate *was* the Roman Governor; and it is, after all, doubtful whether, in faithfulness to their own duties, they could have done otherwise. Must Church and State then slay this Divine Love? Except to the anarchic mystic of the heretical sects, this is a hard saying. For it means that all the proper activities of this outer world combine against Him. It is perhaps enough to say that this, in all likelihood, *will* happen. The mere process of things seems to destroy love—duties and obligations seem to abolish it. It remains certainly an awful warning to the Church lest she cannot recognise the Messias she proclaims; to the State lest the means become the end, and this Divine Contemplation between lovers, which must in the end be one of the chief objects which the State proposes to itself to maintain, be lost and destroyed in its consideration of its own importance; lest the poor be sacrificed to an impossible stability, and Love be crucified lest Caesar should change, or the party-system be abolished.

In some measure or other these four powers seem to combine

---

his analysis, e.g.—John is mystical contemplation; James is service of others; Peter is the profession of religion; Matthew is the business capacity; Thomas is the sceptical intellect; Simon Zelotes is holy anger—and so on. It is in this sense that Judas Iscariot is the mouth of hell and inevitable treachery. [Textual note by Williams]

against him—tyrannical desire, treacherous manners, cares of life, and obtuse religion; the special guilt (whatever that may be) of the lovers and the general stupidity of the world. But though this Passion is so easily, so inevitably brought about, the realization of it is by no means an easy or common state of the soul. It is at the first suggestions of such a Death that many lovers, like the disciples, fly from and deny His Deity; saying, in effect, "If Thou be the Son of God, come down from the cross".[20] This is the same demand which the powers of hell made upon him in the earlier Temptation: the only temptation that can be offered to Almighty God—in some way to produce a contradiction in His nature, to set His Mercy against His Justice, His Compassion against His Inevitability. That the desolation of the disciples, as well as their desertion, is to Him an agony did not and does not compel Him to recede, in the work of redemption or the work of marriage, one step from the slow process of His laws which are Himself.

But all have not forsaken him and fled; the Divine Mother, the elect John, were found by the cross. And the Christian lovers, who have considered within themselves[21] the nature of Love, will have known from the beginning that there is another side to the early delight. To them[22] it is a place of purgation as well as joy; it is in truth a little universe of place and time, of earth, of purgatory, of heaven or hell. The companion in this experience is to him or to her the instrument of fire which shall burn away his corrupt part.

> In me your doom is fixed; I am the place
> And time of your purgation; though that face
> Looked never on me but with high regard
> Of heavenly love, unshaken and unmarred,
> Looked it—you know, and only you can know—
> On Love's interior monitions so?

Love is Holiness and Divine Indignation; the placidity of an ordinary married life is the veil of a spiritual passage into profound things. Nor

20. Matthew 27:40.
21. The typist has read "lover" as "lovers" (either reading is reasonable), and has therefore altered "has" in the MS to "have," and "himself" to "themselves." I read the first word as "lover," in which case "has" and "himself" both stand.
22. The typist has read this word as "them"; I read it as "these."

is this all; the lover knows himself also to be the cross upon which the Beloved is to be stretched, and so she also of her lover. A suggestion of this—probably no more—is to be found merely in the fact of her existence, the sense of being for ever intimately bound to another which when it is not repose is agony, the state of suspension upon a substance alien and unavoidable for which, though from a more dreadful distance, crucifixion is the only comparison. There is no middle state into which this issues—either it is continued into an anguish of entire repulsion and hate, or, by the grace of that Crucifixion which includes it but is so much more than it alone, it becomes itself a purgation and a redemption. This is—in its degree, and who shall say how terrific that degree may become?—the annihilation of the selfhood which the saints have sought, and the end of it is union.

Christ who was born of flesh is manifested in flesh. This is perhaps part of the sacramental grace of marriage, to which so much importance has been attributed and of which so little has been explained. Intercourse between man and woman is, or at least is capable of being, in a remote but real sense, a symbol of the Crucifixion. There is no other human experience, except Death, which so enters into the life of the body; there is no other human experience which so binds the body to another being. The central experience of sanctity is to be so bound to another, though for the saints this other is God. But what of the lover if Love is also God?

> With too cold fire, with too unsteady eyes,
> The poisonous bite of the world to cauterise
> Have those elect hands sought; trouble no more
> Except as Love shall teach you to abhor:
> But if in Him you yield your full consent,
> Then be myself the unhappy instrument
> Of your vast death; too helpless to relent,
> Be stretched upon this cross now; make me one,
> In a most dreadful consecration,
> With all your sin and punishment; retrieve
> In me, in me, your proper way to live,
> And make me your anointed: O in me
> Work out the fairer you that is to be,
> And find that love is one with sanctity!

That all hope of resurrection, save perhaps as a mere intellectual formula, is abolished in this distress is no doubt a necessary part of it. Yet the Resurrection exists, and all things are restored, but the last things are not quite as the first. How profound the Resurrection may be depends on how profound the Crucifixion may have been: it does not, in any case, according to the records of His Humanity, manifest itself as a final state. For the Resurrection is followed by the Ascension, and the Ascension, like the Death, is a departure. Love that was visibly present, a light and a wonder, withdraws himself into the secret and heavenly places; and in His stead there descends upon the lovers the indwelling grace of the Spirit, nourishing and sustaining them. He it is who so maintains a happy marriage, though perhaps a happy marriage in this sense is as rare among marriages as a great saint among orthodox Christians, that he brings to the remembrance of the lovers "all things, whatsoever I have said unto you".[23] "I have yet many things", Christ says to the lovers in their earlier days, "to say unto you, but ye cannot bear them now".[24] But "when the Spirit of truth is come . . . he shall glorify me, for he shall take of mine and show it unto you".[25] It is he, then, that maintains, in other days and through later experiences, all that Love proclaimed at first, and fulfills all that was prophesied. "He shall testify of Me, and ye also shall bear witness because ye have been with me from the beginning."[26]

It is not suggested that, in the life of most lovers, this sequence of states of consciousness proceeds in the same ordered development as the incidents of his earthly life. The Crucifixion, the Resurrection, are eternal facts, dimly regarded, slightly felt, at many different times. Happiness does not always wait to follow the full dereliction; and there are many hints of the Crucifixion, many gleams of the Resurrection, sometimes in the most trifling affairs (but not therefore to be taken less seriously), before the supreme experiences, the dark night and the dawn, are revealed. For (to take one point alone) the life of the lovers in Christ is so intermingled with the life of the Church that this greater life

23. John 14:26.
24. John 16:12.
25. John 16:13-14.
26. John 15:26-27.

illuminates or darkens the lesser. Nor is marriage, even for the married, the necessary way of revelation; there are a myriad others. As there are only a few to whom He communicates His life directly and without earthly, if sacramental, veils, of one kind or another, so there may be only a few to whom He communicates Himself after this manner in marriage. But that the possibility is always there is part of the thesis of Romantic Theology, as the possibility of salvation for all is the thesis of Christian Theology at large. Men will believe in Love enough to risk incredible things, so that to take the appalling chances of marriage is now no more than a convention among us; it is for those who have believed in Him to this extent, who have acknowledged the strength and glory of love, its beauty and its terror; who have heard its word in the speech of the adored, and lost their hearts to it—it is for them to decide upon His own cry:

"He that believeth on me, believeth not on me, but on him that sent me. And he that seeth me seeth not me but him that sent me. I am come a light into the world, that whosoever believeth on me should not abide in darkness. And if any man hear my words and believe not, I judge him not; for I came not to judge the world, but to save the world. He that rejecteth me, and receiveth not my words, hath one that judgeth him; the word that I have spoken, the same shall judge him in the last day."[27]

27. John 12:44-48.

CHAPTER III

The New Testament in Romantic Theology

When the principle laid down in the previous section has been accepted, the application of it to the New Testament must be largely a matter of individual study. It is desirable however that one warning should be insisted upon before a few examples of the method are given—and that is a warning against ingenuity. To the student of an alert mind such ingenuity is one of the chief dangers of the way, and discussion of the safeguard against it will be left to a later section. Here it is only necessary to point out how serious the danger is. Interpretation of texts has often led in other branches of theology to most unhappy results, and though it is difficult to imagine that a time will ever come when ecclesiastical prejudice will exercise itself on behalf of some defined meaning in Romantic Theology, yet even that possibility cannot wholly be ruled out, and meanwhile the danger to the individual is that he should limit some saying or act of our Saviour's to this aspect only. The whole is greater than the part, and the Eternal Son is more than any understanding of him in any of His offices of salvation.

The New Testament consists of inspired records concerning the earthly life of Jesus Christ and of inspired commentaries upon Him. The life of Jesus Christ being also the life of Love in marriage we may take it that these records and commentaries will be no less applicable to that subordinate life. In so far as these records give us the actual process of His life they have been discussed in the last section. Here we are concerned only to note a few of His sayings with this interpretation.

One of the difficulties which historic Christianity has had to avoid, though it has not always succeeded in doing so, has been the suggestion

27

that Christ's words are always the words of an outsider, imposed upon
the world but not immanent in its nature. The relation between the
immanence and transcendence of Almighty God belongs to another
branch of theology. The reason for the difficulty which man experiences
in realising that Christ's sayings are the expression of Life itself, the
actual life which he is living, is that, in general, first, men have no acute
and shapely sense of Life as a whole, and secondly, they do not imagine
Life as identical in the end with Christ. They do not *imagine* it; they
know it, perhaps, with their reasonable minds, or they accept it as a
doctrine. But their experiences of Life are usually so weak, or so
detached from, or (even) so opposed to, all they read in the New
Testament that its unity with that Divine Saviour is remote from their
vision. They are not passionately conscious of it.

Now it is here that the particular experience of marriage comes
in. Nothing is easier than to overrate this experience of love; it is, for
most of us, weak and paltry enough. But it is the most illuminating—not
necessarily the strongest—we have probably ever had, and it is renewed. That is to say, it does not end with the first meeting of the lovers;
it prolongs itself through months and years. It is of a nature to change
definitely (according to our Western conventions) the material side of
a man's life; he actually does leave his father and mother; he involves
himself in setting up a new household. It is, at any rate, something that
happens to him and produces definite results. He is therefore in the
presence of something, namely—love, which can be definitely appreciated. And it is much easier for him to believe that this love has a
separate being and moves according to the laws of its own nature than
to believe that the apparent chaos which he calls Life is capable of any
such existence and expression. Love is shapely and shapes things: life is
(apparently) without form and void. In the one, light—in the other,
darkness—is upon the face of the deep.[1]

Take, for instance, the sayings of Christ about divorce. These to
the Christian romantic are not laws imposed (even for his own good)
upon him by an inventive and almighty Mind contemplating the world.
They are the utterances of Love itself. And the adultery committed in
cases of their breach is not so much against the other lover as against

1. See Genesis 1:2.

Love; for it is in essence the desertion of Him in his progress through life for another teacher. It is as if the Apostles, say on the Saturday after Good Friday, had all by a sudden illumination become Buddhists. (This of course is for those instances where a fresh love really does seem a fresh revelation, and not for the mere sensual drift of the world.) No-one, at least no-one but Christ, could criticise them—but there would be a certain sense that perhaps the coincidence of the disappointment and the new creed was so close as to be regrettable.

But we do not want to be lured away into this aged controversy. Christ himself added to His saying the profound warning when He asserted the indissolubility of marriage. "All men cannot receive this saying, save they to whom it is given. . . . He that is able to receive it, let him receive it" (St. Matthew xix, 11-12).

As another example of His sayings concerning His nature may be taken the phrase which lies behind all our serial stories and novels in which two lovers undergo trials and injuries: "Think not that I am come to send peace on earth: I come not to send peace, but a sword. For I am come to set a man at variance against his father, and the daughter against her mother, and the daughter in law against her mother in law. And a man's foes shall be they of his own household. He that loveth father or mother more than me is not worthy of me: and he that loveth son or daughter more than me is not worthy of me."[2]

If these sayings are true of religion they are also most assuredly true of marriage. And it is in no sense a joke but a quite serious theological comment if we add that of all the genuine familiarity with Christian ideas which in the Middle Ages allowed humour to link itself with religion, our only legacy to-day is in the universal—the vulgar, in the better sense as well as the worse—assumption that a mother-in-law and a daughter-in-law will not get on together: we might even add that the universal joke about a man and his mother-in-law derives from the same fact and is the expression in another medium of those august and terrible words.

Again there are many sayings, especially all those which speak of Christ's unity with His disciples, which, however profoundly true they are of the religious life, must be to most men a hope only, if not a mere

2. Matthew 10:34-37.

dream, instead of having that almost obvious truth to which He seems to appeal, *unless* they are also true of Him in this lesser way. Doubtless it should be the aim of all men, the experience of all, to know them true in religion. But doubtless numbers of the most faithful do not so know them true. But thousands have known them in marriage. "I am come a light into the world, that whosoever believeth in me should not abide in darkness."[3] Or when He disputed with the Jews: "Say ye of him, whom the Father hath sanctified, and sent into the world, Thou blasphemest; because I said, I am the Son of God? If I do not the works of my Father, believe me not. But if I do, though ye believe not me, believe the works: that ye may know, and believe, that the Father is in me, and I in him."[4]

What works are these that they should convince us, remote from Him, that the Father is in him and he in the Father? Miracles? The miracles of Judaea or the miracles of Lourdes? Alas, miracles are only appreciated—save in their subjects, perhaps rarely in the spectators—by the intellectual forces of man, and these do not convert the soul. But beauty, but energy, but charity,[5] but faith, but devotion, but purity, but joy, but peace—these produced, for however short a moment, in a man's being so that he can never doubt that they were, so that they exist maintaining the lover and the beloved in themselves, and suddenly and without his own labours, in a world of utter confusion, these words[6] are they which make a man say with the disciples—"By this we believe that thou camest forth from God."[7] "Thou art the Christ, the Son of the living God.[8] *

There are other sayings which, without this interpretation, have for us hardly even an intellectual appeal: as for example, the answer to

3. John 12:46.
4. John 10:36-38.
5. John Pellow queried whether this word in the typescript should not be "clarity." Having myself now seen the MS, I agree.
6. I judge "words" to be a mistyping of the original "works."
7. John 16:30.
8. Matthew 16:16.

* It is wiser perhaps to confine this preliminary discussion strictly to the Canonical Scriptures; otherwise, one might remark the absolute fitness to this interpretation of the Logion ["*Logia*: A supposed collection of the sayings of Christ which circulated in the early Church" (*Oxford Dictionary of the Christian Church*, p. 833).—ED. NOTE] discovered in 1903—"His disciples say unto him, When wilt thou be manifest to us, and when shall we see thee? He saith, When ye shall be stripped and not be ashamed", or

the Pharisees, which normally seems hardly more than a debating score: "What think ye of Christ? whose son is he?" "The Son of David." "How then doth David in spirit call Him Lord? . . . If David then call him Lord, how is He his son?"[9] This can surely mean little to us, until the delighted gaiety of the lovers hears it. For they very well know how possible it is to be at once the source and servants of this Divine principle. Love is assuredly born of them, and is their son. But assuredly also the parents call the son Lord—being (to borrow another phrase) "In the Spirit on the Lord's day".[10]

So we might go on working through the New Testament text by text, without ingenuity but without fear, discerning more of the nature of the Son of God, by the help of the Catholic Church and of the ladies who are her sisters. But it seems better to leave this now to the individual student, and to devote a few pages to the consideration of the lovers themselves in relation to Christ.

It will be clear that, if and in so far as Christ is to be identified with love and His life with marriage, then and to an equal degree the two lovers stand for the disciples, and the whole company of the faithful, i.e., the Catholic Church. All the warnings that have been offered in reference to the principal identification hold true also of its corollary. The Church is a synthesis of much more than the two lovers; nevertheless no two lovers but correspond in some small way with everything in her. Doubtless, if some evil fortune made a choice between the Church and the Beloved inevitable, he would be the wiser and greater man who remained faithful to the Church; but he who followed the other way, in good faith and good will, would not be outside its graces.

The conversion of the lovers may have been accomplished in many ways. It may have been by the courteous response of Love to a courteous curiosity, as to Andrew and Philip: "Where dwellest thou?" "Come and see."[11] It may have been a sudden summons to a careless

---

of that other which says: "Let not him who seeks cease until he finds, and when he finds he shall be astonished; astonished he shall reach the kingdom, and having reached the kingdom he shall rest." Astonishment, government, rest—are not these the graces of romantic love? [Textual note by Williams]

9. Matthew 22:42-45.
10. Revelation 1:10.
11. John 1:38-39.

mind occupied in ordinary affairs, as to Matthew: "Follow me."[12] It may have been the apocalyptic summons to a mind absorbed in its own obstinacy for good or evil; the Pharisee, the Manichaean,[13] the sensualist, the philanderer may have been thus challenged and overwhelmed on their victorious road to Damascus: "Saul, Saul, why persecutest thou me? . . . I am JESUS, Whom thou persecutest."[14]

By whatever means, the lover has been brought to the consciousness of Him: conversion takes place, or the New Birth, a nativity of the lover as of Love. For the life of the Church is one with the life of Christ, is indeed that life seen in its operations rather than in itself, and the life of the married lovers is in the same way the life of their common Lord. But there is at first a difference for it is the business of marriage as of the Catholic Church to draw its members into closer and closer communion with that which is its principle. And as the Blessed Virgin was for a time "herself the New Testament and the Church",[15] so each lover will see in his or her opposite the gifts and graces with which Christ has endowed His Church—though perhaps as a general rule the Church as a whole seems to correspond more to the woman, and the more limited official priesthood to the man. There are marriages as there are periods when the priesthood seems to be the whole thing, and the Church is a nonentity beside it: marriages and periods of peculiar deadness.

Each sacrament, in a sense, contains within itself all others, and marriage so contains them—not so that they should be neglected, but that by their outward practice in the Catholic life they should be felt, renewed, and developed in the life of marriage. For all the sacraments mean renewal in one way or another: and love perhaps most visibly creates that renewal in the phenomenal world. In the exhausting weariness which is the chief disease of man's soul, and by which the eyes of the physical body have been so disastrously affected, the most comfortable sacrament of the appearance and caress of the Beloved

12. Matthew 9:9.
13. Manichaeanism "was based on a supposed primeval conflict between light and darkness," combined with ascetic beliefs (*Oxford Dictionary of the Christian Church*, p. 864).
14. Acts 9:4-5.
15. Unidentified quotation.

convey most repose, most refreshment. In the dulness of speech which governs us—except for the utterances of the holy poets—it is the speech of the Beloved which so often moves in the accents of eternity. It is, probably, a common experience with most lovers to marvel at the curious propinquity in the talk of the Beloved of the most shattering stupidities with the most profound and revealing truths. At one moment she will talk like a . . . but there is no analogy; at another like one inspired by God. This indeed is the Infallibility of the Church: who talks sometimes like an Archdeacon and sometimes like a god.*

In a similar way is the indefectibility of the Church manifested in the lovers. Mysteriously faithful among all her iniquities, the Church still contains an immaculate centre; and so the Beloved mysteriously remains at once immaculate in love and extremely maculate in everything else. She is, or she seems, miraculously preserved from sin in this alone. And as she, so to her the lover: in the mutual exchange of contemplative delight which we call love.

But this immaculacy, this infallibility, this indefectibility, is not of itself enough. It is the business of the lovers, as of the visible Church, to attain perfection, by being wholly united with their Lord, by "growing" in St. Paul's phrase, into "the stature of the fullness of Christ".[16] And for this the rites and doctrines of the Church contain sufficient instruction, at any rate until the lovers become so much one with their Lord that He mystically instructs them Himself. It may normally be taken for granted that this point will not be reached in this life; in any rare cases where it is reached it will make itself wholly clear. But in general the lovers should regard themselves as part of and subordinated to the life and habits of the Universal Church.

It is not without significance here that the incident of the Woman of Samaria may be quoted. The soul which meets our Lord in the way is reminded of "all things that ever she did",[17] and even while she gives Him to drink from her own vessel of water she is told, "Thou hast had

* The present writer has often wondered that this analogy has never been urged by controversialists on behalf of the Infallibility of the Roman See. It is probably because such controversialists are too often sentimentally inclined to see profundity in all its sayings, and they inevitably suffer for it. [Textual note by Williams]

16. Ephesians 4:13.
17. See John 4:29.

five husbands; and he whom thou now hast is not thy husband".[18] In the eyes of Christ marriage is not, at any rate in its first stages, a final rest. This is the correspondence to the warning of Simeon in the life of Love.

The watchword then for all lovers, in whatever state of marriage they may find themselves, is simply the old phrase, upon which so much scorn has been cast, to be "in love with Love".[19] But this is not to be taken sentimentally or over-solemnly. It means in effect that they should carry themselves always as if in presence of this Stranger, desiring to learn more of him, accepting anything that happens as a necessary result of His life in a perverted world; of which perversion they themselves are a part, save for some few moments in this Divine relationship alone. There may be some of us who in the end will have no purer or more perfect life to show than those moments in which we waited for our lovers; nor are those moments less holy because of the delight that often mingles with them, nor less truthful because they may often have seemed to prophesy a delight which was not always, when she came, entirely fulfilled. For He withdraws Himself sometimes in her presence, retiring a little and leaving her to work her own instruction on our souls. No doubt this retirement is from a thousand causes,—weariness or ill-temper or pain or worry. But again He is equally present in sudden unexpected moments, and it is the neglect of these moments that is the most fruitful source of disbelief in Him.

Meditation upon such moments then, and the practice of the Christian rites, are two of the means by which the appearance of love and beauty that is at first revealed may be both achieved individually and found to be indeed reality in the lover's companion in love. Something will be said in the next section of the supreme Rite. Here all that need be added is to remind students that in ordinary married life the meals they share, are (in common with all other parts of that experience) sacramental. It is not merely a pleasing emotion that stirs in their hearts when they breakfast or dine with each other; fortunately, since, as in all religion, the emotion is apt unhappily to disappear when

18. John 4:18.
19. Perhaps from St. Augustine's *Confessions*, book III, chapter 1: *amans amare*, "in love with loving."

too much reliance is put on it. Here, as in the Eucharist itself, whatever the emotion, the imagination is capable of belief and assertion; and the lover, at the most unfortunate breakfast, may be allowed to smile a little to himself at the contrast between his feelings and his creed, while he murmurs (as St. Clement taught him): "Where two or three are gathered together in thy Name, there art thou in the midst of them".[20] Morality is to him (as perhaps it should be to all of us in its widest applications) a matter of courtesy, and sullenness over such a breakfast may be a worse sin than adultery. But all these sins were foreseen and endured and purged. Love has undergone all rebuffs and all persecutions; and behold, he is not there, he is risen.[21] Many a lover must be able to recall incidents of which, though for his own pride he might wish that they could be abolished, he would not choose to lose the memory because of their dear poignancy. But he desires intensely that they should not be repeated: here (as in so many other things) that which is but a matter of dull and half-hearted resolution in religion is a matter of sharp experience in love. Many a slanderer, many a thief, though mildly regretting his slander or theft, has a real difficulty in seeing it as an offence against God. He knows it is, as one knows that Uganda is in Central Africa, and, consequently, with as much effect on his daily life. But he knows that he has wounded the heart of this Love, that he has blinded it and bound it, and knows at the same time that it is altogether powerful and free. The Crucifixion and the Resurrection exist; and in a passionate adoration of that Love which is manifest in both at once, or rather of which both are modes of manifestation (since things are what they are), he can approach the centre of this Divine Mystery. It is perhaps in this sense that the Love of marriage exclaims to him, smitten with a palsy and a stranger in his home, "But that ye may know that the Son of Man hath power on earth to forgive sins, I say unto thee, Arise, and take up thy bed, and go into thy house".[22]

And, incredible wonder of love! there *is* the house, there *is* the Beloved.

20. See Matthew 18:20.
21. See Luke 24:6.
22. Mark 2:10-11.

CHAPTER IV

The Mass in Romantic Theology

The discussion of the Mass in this science is a discussion of two things: (1) the intention, (2) the ritual. It will be convenient to indicate briefly the possibilities of the first before proceeding to some application of the second.

The intention with which the lover hears Mass will vary probably at different points in the process of marriage. It will be understood that communion is the hearing of mass fulfilled and put into extreme action, and is therefore covered by the same laws. It will be understood further that as nothing in the identification of the life of Christ with marriage derogates from, but rather increases the sense of, the general and universal truths of that life, so nothing in this particular method of hearing Mass detracts from its high mystery as a means and symbol of universal salvation. No additional meaning discovered in it reduces its position in the general life of all Christians.

There are, then, as was hinted by that great doctor of this science, Coventry Patmore, two chief methods of hearing mass for the student. And though these two methods may be used alike at any point in marriage, and should so be used, nevertheless one is more appropriate to the earlier, the other to the later stages.

"The Blessed Sacrament," said Patmore, "is first of all a symbol of the beloved; afterwards the beloved is a symbol of the Blessed Sacrament." Such a pregnant saying has conceived within it the whole of Romantic Theology, and perhaps hardly needs amplification. In the intense experience of the birth of love, it is hardly to be wondered at, and (if this science is right) it is most just, that the Sacrament which he accepts mentally to be that of the Divine Humanity, the Body and Blood of the Saviour, should appear to the lover to be closely related to that glorious body of his lady through which he apprehends divine things. To identify them were too much; it is Love, and not the mother of Love, who draws the world into Himself in mass and communion. But he who is present at the celebration with the thought in his mind of Christ who is Love, and bearing in his mind also the contemplation of that lady who is the source of love in him will inevitably regard Christ primarily in this manner of His life. His intention will be that this love shall so order the circumstances of this life of marriage that he and his lady may be made one in the grace of that divine contemplation. Eternity itself will be hinted to him in the sense which will strengthen within him that in such contemplation lies the centre of love: that, as the beloved herself appears, love is without before and after, and of it (as of God) all that can be said is I am that I am.[1] More also is true. The Body of Christ is, in a hidden but assured way, one with the bodies of his saints—that is, with all true lovers. But this is in eternity, and it is with eternity that the body of his lady is seen to be illustrious. It is therefore that eternal body which he at once knows himself, and yet desires, to be contemplating; and this consciousness provides him with food for his exile, though it may make that exile more bitter, and may in some sense injure his ordinary relationship with her. For no belief in the dogmas of Romantic Theology will make ordinary give-and-take between two sensitive human natures an easy thing, any more than a belief in Dogmatic Theology makes it easier to be courteous to a man who has trodden on one's toe in a railway queue. It is here that the otherness of the beloved is to be felt; and as it is one of the difficulties of marriage that that otherness is so acute, so it is one of its graces that it is delightedly accepted.

But, admirable as this manner of hearing mass is for the elementary student, it is not that which he should desire. Strictly speaking however the second method belongs to Mystical Theology, for it is concerned with communion with God. It is rather, in the later life, without church, or in the earlier parts of the Rite, that the beloved plays her part. The slow approach to the beloved gives place to a slow

1. Exodus 3:14.

37

recoil. Love, which in the earlier stages appeared to intensify her love and her beauty, now thrusts itself between them. The road into eternity is found to be strait and to involve the turning of the attention from that lady who was earlier its sole means of manifestation. Such is the teaching of the doctors, and to them and to the mystics of the Church the student must be referred, though a further suggestion may be offered towards the end of this section.

We come to the ritual, which opens with the Lord's Prayer and a Collect. The Lord's Prayer is that taught by Christ to all his disciples, of whatever vocation, and its petitions are of the broadest application.[2] It is addressed to the Father and Source of Love, and the first three clauses (following on the supreme assertion that he is in heaven, whatever and wherever that heaven may be) are not to be interpreted too closely by any individual experience; although equally no hint is to be allowed to escape, and it is the Will which is done in the heavenly relationship of the lovers which is also to be done in the world without. The last four petitions have their special application. It is the bread of strength (not the wine of rapture) bestowed in love; the tender forgiveness, which is almost too intimate and dear an experience to bear the word 'forgiveness'; the deliverance from temptations and evils incident to love; for which the lover prays. Similarly in the Collect, the petition is first, that the imagination may be lit "by the inspiration of thy Holy Spirit, that we may perfectly love thee, through Jesus Christ our Lord."[3] Understood so, it appears not so incredible a task that those imaginations which are now at once the children and parents of Jesus Christ should move on through Him to his Father and theirs: "to whom all hearts are open, all desires known, and from whom no secrets are hid," because he is himself the final Simplicity of each heart, to whom they have at this time perhaps more closely reached, in the lucid simplicity of love, than ever before.

In the English Use of the Catholic Church, the two preliminary

---

2. See Matthew 6:9-13.

3. This collect from the Communion Service of the Church of England's Book of Common Prayer reads in full as follows: "Almighty God, unto whom all hearts be open, all desires known, and from whom no secrets are hid: Cleanse the thoughts of our hearts by the inspiration of thy Holy Spirit, that we may perfectly love thee, and worthily magnify thy Holy Name; through Christ our Lord. Amen."

prayers are followed by the Ten Commandments.[4] They stand here, where morality should stand, at the beginning of the religious way—in no sense the process, much less the end, but a necessary preliminary, and a preliminary capable of ever further and further transmutations as the postulant proceeds upon his road. The division in purport between the four earlier and the six later is maintained in Romantic Theology; the four declaring the proper rights of God, the six maintaining those of our neighbours, who is in this interpretation the Beloved herself. The first and the last are the two supreme pronouncements. The first, retaining its general meaning, is capable now of the more particular one that the lover who desires to follow this way must especially deny all other gods: even, as the second commandment goes on to insist, his own ideas of Love. "Thou shalt *not* make to thyself the likeness of anything"—not Love in the heavens above, or the Beloved in the Earth beneath. It is not so much to intellectual ideas that this refers, as to a state of soul which rests upon some self-created phantasy and does not lay itself wholly open to the Otherness from himself, the not-himself-ness, of the approaching Power, divine or human. It is from this limiting state that the lover desires, after every commandment, to be freed; and it is with peculiar propriety that the Warning is offered to him: "I visit the sins of the fathers upon the children", since it is the very principle which brings forth children that is here darkly revealing its nature.

The third commandment sets a seal upon the lips of the lover, but it is perhaps the one most easily broken. The name of this just but austere Deity, this jealous and omnipotent God, is used for every degree of mild affection. The name of God is not profaned by the most ribald oaths as the name of Love is profaned by the most conventional assumptions. Mankind to-day pronounces that word, like the gentleman in Mr. Chesterton's novel, as if it were saying 'boots'; whereas it should be used only when something of its own eternal sovereignty is felt to exist. It might almost be urged that from this point of view, the three purposes for which marriage was ordained, according to the Book of Common Prayer—viz. for the procreation of children, as a remedy against sin,

---

4. See Exodus 20:1-17. In the following discussion, Williams is following the Communion Service of the Church of England's Book of Common Prayer, quoting from it rather than the Authorized Version of the Bible.

and for mutual help and comfort—are something terribly like taking His Name in vain. For what are all these but accidental graces—in view of that first commandment which dominates the rest—"*I am the Lord thy God: thou shalt have none other Gods but Me.*"

It is as something of a safeguard against this guilt that the fourth commandment comes, where the lover is bidden see that for the seventh part of his time he rests from all kinds of labour and keeps it holy to the Lord. This consecration of the week-end, or at least the greater part of it, to repose and contemplation of the beloved, is thus seen to be—not a mere amusing habit of young lovers—but a duty imposed upon all her married children by the Catholic Church. It is, curiously enough, one of the most difficult to obey; but the Parable of the Sower is another warning against its neglect, of which the roadway, the stones, the shallow ground, are the inevitable result.[5]

Such then are the laws by which Deity safeguards its own possibility of functioning and destroys that unbelief which hinders His mighty works. The next—"Honour thy father and mother"—refers the lover to the great teachers of this science, though in Romantic Theology it supplies at any rate a fortunate few with a reason for honouring their actual father and mother which other departments of the science have perhaps a little neglected. For to those few their parents are like ministers and manifestations of Love with themselves, the closest, the most evident, teachers and examples of it. And this new land, this country of delight, "which the Lord thy God giveth thee", and which is none other than "thy God" himself, may very well become a native country to those who respect its inhabitants, and their days be long in it. Otherwise the commandment would seem to refer to such doctors of the science as will be briefly mentioned in the next section, and to the Catholic Church as its supreme exponent.

The remaining five commandments are on the whole concerned to maintain the sacredness of the Beloved herself. The tenth is the greatest—for here she is definitely set free from a too tyrannical possession: whether "thy neighbour" refers to her, as some think, or, as others, to God. If these last students are right, then the beloved is His house and His wife, and all her various activities and properties are

5. See Matthew 13:1-23.

governed by the other clauses. In any case this law is a very strict limitation of personal desire of any kind: it is few lovers whose intimacy with and contemplation of the beloved are entirely free from "covetousness", and in many it spreads to include all those aspects of her being which were never intended to be theirs.

For the rest, murder and theft, adultery and false witness expand and repeat the second commandment. They are states of mind following on a refusal to admit absolute Otherness, turnings back upon the lover's own dreams and preferences. False witness is especially dangerous, for false witness (it must be remembered) need not necessarily be derogatory. The lover who deliberately cheats himself into a belief in his lady's unreal perfections—who believes her to be tactful when she is clumsy, or good-tempered when she is irritable, or industrious when she is lazy, is as certainly bearing false witness as he who deliberately slanders her. If he honestly believes these things he is of course morally innocent (though perhaps intellectually weak), but to blind himself to the facts is one of the things that the Love of marriage never forgives. It leads to the murder of truth, the theft of delight, the adultery with illusions and sentimentalities; in the end, to the making and worshipping of a lie—the lie of the lover's own selfhood blindly contented with itself.

The preliminary rules of morality are rehearsed, and the lover hearing Mass has reminded himself of them. The Ritual begins to approach its business, by the slightly unexpected means of a prayer for "thy chosen servant George, our King and Governor."[6] It is not altogether so out of place as it sounds. For what is to happen? The lover at Mass has to remember that marriage, though pre-eminent, is only *one* of the means of Christ's revelation. Love is drawing himself in, as it were, bearing his children with him, from all those means towards the central mystery. In the prayers for the King (and, with him, for the community), in the offertory, and in the prayer for the whole state of Christ's Church militant here on earth, the lover is reminded of this. Whatever rites he keeps in his own private devotions—of marriage or friendship or art or science or sport or politics—he is to pray now for all these schools and guilds in the Church of Love militant upon earth, that the Universal

6. In this prayer for the Sovereign the name is kept up-to-date. When *Outlines of Romantic Theology* was written, the Sovereign was King George V.

Church may be inspired with the spirit of truth, unity, and concord. He repeats the Creed, therefore, as do all the congregation in their separate vocations, not in the terminology of that vocation, but in the larger and more universally applicable language of the historic Christ. This certainly he may apply to his own subordinate life, as he may apply the Offertory Sentences, but the greater is to include the lesser. Of these Sentences, as of the Epistle and Gospel, not much need be said, since the discussion of the New Testament in the last section covers them. One or two may be quoted: e.g.—the first: "Let your light—your love—so shine before men that they may see your good works, and glorify your Father which is in heaven";[7] "Not every one that saith unto me, Love, love, shall enter into the Kingdom of heaven";[8] "If I have sown unto you spiritual things (it is the Beloved speaking), is it a great matter if I shall reap your worldly things?"[9] "While we have time, let us do good unto all men; and specially unto such as are of the household of faith"[10]—i.e., peculiarly the beloved herself. Nevertheless, the emphasis is for awhile now upon the "all men".

The Invitation however will again appeal to the lover most immediately through his sense of marriage. There he is in love and charity with his neighbour, there he is leading a new life, and walking from henceforth in God's holy ways. And it is for increase of comfort in the ways that he treads round the most sacred beauty of his lady, ways of the world that appear to him for perhaps the first time really holy, that he is to receive "this Holy Sacrament". He glimpses something of the truth conveyed in the Comfortable Words; but he is again united, this time not with the Church militant alone, but with all the company of heaven, when he enters, through the Proper Preface and the arch-angelic trisagion,[11] upon the mystery of Christ Incarnate, by whom the

7. Matthew 5:16. The words "your love" are, of course, Williams's interpolation.
8. Matthew 7:21. Williams has substituted the words "Love, love" for "Lord, Lord."
9. See 1 Corinthians 9:11.
10. Galatians 6:10.
11. *Trisagion*: Greek for "three times holy," a chant found in all ancient liturgies. In the Communion Service of the Book of Common Prayer it appears (hence Williams's phrase, "arch-angelic trisagion") as: "Therefore with angels and archangels, and with all the company of heaven, we laud and magnify thy glorious Name, evermore praising thee, and saying: Holy, holy, holy, Lord God of hosts; heaven and earth are full of thy glory; glory be to thee, O Lord most high."

Universal Sacrament of Communion and the particular sacrament of marriage exists. In the prayer of Humble Approach he may remember again how the body of the Beloved seems to him transfused with the Divine Body, how Christ Incarnate is almost visibly made one with her, how his own sinful body is made clean and his own soul washed through that Body and Blood.

There follow the Consecration and Communion.

The central mystery of the Mass has been at all times the subject of dream and speculation, of theology and devotion. If it is the centre of Christian life, it is, also and therefore, the centre of all life—anyhow on this planet, and perhaps everywhere. For the mystery of the Redemption—of which this is the sign and means—lies close to the mystery of Creation. The Sacrifice of the Crucifixion was the unmaking of all life that it should be remade after the great original pattern; a deliberate unmaking instead of an inevitable decay. So far as chaos could come again upon a world in which God was immanent, so far in that darkness it came; wounding and overwhelming the Sacred Body, inclosing and darkening the Sacred Spirit within. It is in the nature of Omnipotence always to be able to endure more and to go farther than the utmost that can be brought against him; and perhaps this is the nature of the last Judgement, that He leaves to every man the choice of dealings with Him. If a man will shape his life upon a basis of pride and anger, then he shall find a greater pride and anger in God; if he is covetous and robs others, God shall be covetous and rob him; if he is full of love, then God shall be full of love. The Mass is an invisible communication, not only of redemption but also of creation and judgement: it is an absorption of the communicant in his degree into eternity. It is therefore above all things the relation between his own soul and Love with which the lover is concerned; and though he passes into the mystery by the channels which Love has prepared, Love itself issues therefrom in all his terrible strength along the channels which the lover has prepared. It is in this sense that he too may "eat and drink his own damnation";[12] for what his sincerity brings will certainly be strengthened, desire or covetousness or humility or pride or sentimentality. But it is also here that he is renewed, confirmed, and ordained. He is renewed with—or

12. Third Exhortation in the Communion Service: "we eat and drink our own damnation."

rather there are renewed in him—those graces of the First and Second Creation (the Second itself but a renewing of the First) which manifest Christ to the beloved; he is confirmed in Christ who is their love, and drawn inwards into a further consciousness of Him; he is ordained to his office of priest and mediator. Such an office he may well be advised himself to neglect; he will say *Nolo episcopari,* [13] and forget even that he holds that office. For if the ordinary priesthood have tended to err in taking themselves too solemnly, it will be absolute damnation for the lover to begin consciously to mediate the graces revealed in him—except by such decencies as dressing as well as he can, as punctuality, courtesy, devotion. His priesthood will be the more effective if he makes it but a glass of love.

This priesthood has no doubt its general business in the ordinary domestic occupations of married life, and is more particularly realised—his by her, and hers by him—in those moments of astonished delight which recur, rarely perhaps and at a distance, but assuredly, during the course of such life. But it has also a more particular act. As communion is the means of the larger religious life, so it is also of the lesser; communion in a sacramental act, reception of sacramental nourishment. In neither case is it, if hindered or prevented by lawful and holy reasons, necessary to salvation; but it is, in both cases, generally necessary. In that intercourse which is usually referred to as the consummation of marriage* the presence of Love, that is, of Christ, is sacramentally imparted by each to the other. If this act is not capable of being a sacrament, then it is difficult to see in what way marriage itself is more sacramental than any other occupation; and its inclusion in that group of rites which have the Eucharist as their crown is undeserved. Nothing more is signified by such an inclusion than that God bestows upon the lovers graces sufficient for them to do well in their vocation, as, it must be believed, he does on all men at all times everywhere.

---

13. "I do not wish to be made a bishop," said by St. Ambrose. Born in 339, the son of a Roman official, Ambrose studied law and later became governor of the district around Milan. Not yet baptized, he was a catechumen—one studying Christianity—when the Bishop of Milan suddenly died. In spite of his protests, within a few days Ambrose had been baptized, ordained priest, and consecrated Bishop of Milan.

* It is of course nothing of the sort; at best it is the channel by which a deeper marriage is instituted; the consummation, however it may be in this act signified, foretold, and hastened, is usually far away in the Divine Life. [Textual note by Williams]

But if the communion which is below is indeed a symbol of and means to the communion which is above, if the Christ of the Eucharist and the Love of the marriage-night are indeed not two but one, if the devout and Catholic lover bestows and receives more than either he desires or deserves—the Real Presence of the Most Sacred Body and Blood, then certainly marriage has been rightly if darkly honoured by the whole Church, for it is a very real part of the communication of Himself by Christ to the Church, which is its life. Here also the work of sanctification is carried on, and that mysterious reality—the Body of the Resurrection—may already be shaped and nourished throughout the sacred bodies of the lovers.

Enough stress has probably been laid already on the fact that it is not necessarily desirable for the lover to have this office of his always in his mind when he approaches the altar. There is always a danger, in the weakness of man, that he should limit the greater by the lesser; and the Mystery of the Eucharist was not designed for the needs and opportunities of marriage alone. The most married of lovers has a hundred other affairs and relationships in his life to the proper fulfilling of which the graces of this sacrament are necessary. It is the whole life, not only a part of it, even though the most significant part, which is to be offered to and to be absorbed by Christ; and all that life is to be, in the end, identified with Him. As a matter of practice, therefore, the lover will probably be wise to meditate upon the particular teachings of Romantic Theology "outside church" or during the opening ceremonies of the Mass, but when the Canon has been begun to put away so far as possible all methods of interpretation, and to keep only the intention to let the work of Love be fully accomplished in him. But it is permitted to, and even urged upon, the Christian that he should make intercession especially at this time for all mankind, especially those who are dear to him; and there will be therefore for him a particular meaning in the prayer which follows the Communion—"Thou dost . . . assure us thereby . . . that we are very members incorporate in the mystical body of thy Son, which is the blessed company of all faithful people. . . . And we most humbly beseech thee, O heavenly Father, so to assist us with thy grace, that we may continue in that holy fellowship, and do all such good works as thou has prepared for us to walk in, through Jesus Christ our Lord."

45

What the "continuance in that holy fellowship", pushed to its difficult, unfamiliar, but predestined end, might achieve it is difficult to imagine. In the records of Christian sanctity, there have been celibate saints and married saints. But are there any records of lovers who are also saints in virtue of their consciousness of that love? What, lacking any records of that experience, may we not dream of the high triumphs of any two lovers who knew that their love was Christ, that their marriage was His life, and pursued him in holy fellowship together? Nothing less than this is the suggestion of the Mass, and the promise of their success is in it also. Remote beyond our present apprehension, except dimly, lies even the beginning of that Way, though it may have been followed (without perhaps the intellectual formulation) in many obscure households. The mystic who lives in the loneliest solitude of prayer and vigil is yet one with the whole fellowship of the Church; and so each of two lovers, though seeming often solitary, may be one with a royal companion. It may be that, of all ways to the heights, this, once it is known, may prove the easiest and swiftest, so far as any such way can be easy or swift. For of all those mystical paths this seems to be the one in which at the beginning the End is most clearly seen: here he is known to be alpha and omega, the first and the last. If the lovers abide in him at the beginning as Man and God, human and divine, how easy, how natural, should be their growth with Him into the full consciousness of Divinity and its full possession; and what other food could be theirs during that growth than this most blessed Body and Blood? This too is the growth which is desired in the first Collect of the Rite, "that we may perfectly love thee . . . through Jesus Christ our Lord".

And since Love and Christ are one, and the work of redemption, formation, and union is one with his dealings with man in whatever state He is known, it may even be that the operation of this work takes place for some by means of their marriage. There are souls to whom religion is not much more than a mere formal duty, if that, who are yet capable of heroic achievements in love, of temptation and crucifixion in marriage if not in the Church. Vigil and fast, devotion and self-surrender, are aimed in the end at one sole End, and holiness may be reached by the obvious ways as well as by the more secret. The years of marriage may even have removed almost all memory of the high genesis

46

of marriage, and the altar may be "to an unknown God",[14] for the name of his deity is forgotten. In the devotion of many a wife and many a husband, when the evils of the world are upon them, Christ redeems them and draws them to himself; they are upon the cross none the less because they offer it in churches but a merely casual knee. "He is received perfectly and entire under either species", and though it seems in accord with the Divine intention that the faithful should communicate under both, yet the work of salvation is not hindered by the adoption of the other method, though perhaps its consciousness may be. But this is a matter for the expert theologian.

And, to refer again to the matter of divorce, it is because marriage is a means of the work of redemption that two lovers in whom it has been begun are required by the Church to submit themselves to that work to the end. Divorce is an attempt to nullify a sacrament actually in operation; as if a man should attempt to begin the supernatural life by being rebaptised. It is not that it ought not to happen; for Christians it cannot happen, whatever formula is pronounced or ceremonial enacted. When the work is once begun, for better or worse it cannot be stopped. Nevertheless, it may very well happen, through the frailty of man, that the process of reconciliation by the Church and the process by marriage do not effectively coincide. Marriage may have been a formal matter and the religious experience of love may take place afterwards between one of the pair and some outside third. It is difficult to see how, in such a case, any other arrangement can be come to than that the lovers should make a formal choice between the Church and the new experience. It does not perhaps in the end matter very much which, if the choice is honestly made, but no good can come from the attempt to impose either upon the other. In the nature of things salvation demands an utter surrender, which is just what the known possibility of divorce prevents and forbids.

After this, the Mass, having as it were nothing more to say or do, passes hastily to its end; repeating the Lord's Prayer with a deeper significance than before, reminding the lover in the *Gloria*[15] how he

14. Acts 17:23.
15. The anthem near the end of the Communion Service which begins "Glory be to God on high."

47

may have understood by his own experience—though but for an hour—something of what is meant by those most happy words, "Thou that takest away the sins of the world". For it is among the highest of the graces of romantic love that it lifts its servants not only out of weariness but out of sin, setting them for some few heart-beats above all desire of greed and mischief, in the experience of a lovely content.

"The peace of God, which passeth all understanding, keep your hearts and minds in the knowledge and love of God, and of His Son Jesus Christ our Love."[16]

16. Part of the blessing at the end of the Communion Service. Williams has substituted "Love" for "Lord."

CHAPTER V

Dangers and Safeguards

Reference has already been made to the chief dangers which attend the student of Romantic Theology, and they are brought together for a brief discussion only that they may be accentuated. They are not perhaps different in kind from those which await any student of Theology, but (as with other similarities) they are on this particular side more easily discernible. They are ingenuity and sentimentality—to which might be added infidelity, were it not that this is a danger attached to all committals and all resolutions.

Ingenuity and sentimentality are, in effect, the same thing: viz. occupation with the means rather than the End, and with the emotion or the thought rather than the living Principle. But the first is, on the whole, intellectual; the second, on the whole, emotional. Ingenuity arises from the delight—in its own degree a perfectly just delight—taken by an active mind in working out parallels between the symbol and the thing symbolised: or (in this particular matter) detecting points of identification. Once the idea has been accepted, such a mind asks nothing better than to work out the details. It is generally in something of a hurry; it is always restless until every conceivable word and incident has been fitted into the scheme. This concentration on the symbol—for, in spite of its pleasant pretence, the concentration of the ingenious mind is always on the symbol and never on the fullness of symbol and symbolised—this concentration brings its own reward. The reward is the gradual death of all living meaning, the substitution of appearances for realities, of industrious toil at a jig-saw puzzle for the living recognition of a friend's face.

The student who is anxious to avoid this trap will remind himself that in patience and confidence shall be his strength. If he sees reason to believe that Romantic Theology is indeed a true branch of this most high science, that Immanuel lives indeed in this city of mortal love, he will take up his own lodging there, keep his religious duties and wait. It is no use instituting a text-to-text visitation; theology has already suffered enough from such methods. The kingdom of heaven may suffer violence, but it never yet for a single moment suffered, much less allowed itself to be taken by, a niggling curiosity. The light that light-eneth every man that cometh into the world[1] is capable of doing its own enlightenment at its own time; and God forbid that any student of Romantic Theology should become a too-ingenious proselytiser either of others or, more subtly and more dangerously, of himself. Passion, and the whole of this science demands and assumes passion as its very life, cannot do fretwork with words; though it is capable of sitting down in worshipping silence to the study of every detail in the vast repository of the Gospels. What passion hears at the Mass or in the Lessons, is to be trusted (so long as it is in accord with the whole teaching of the Catholic Church); nothing else, at any time, in any place, by any body.

Nevertheless, passion is not sentimentality. The ingenious mind meandering among texts is a close friend of the ingenious body meandering among emotions. If the fellowship of our fair lord Love is to become a group of self-indulgent phantasts, it had been better that Dante himself should have had a millstone tied round his neck and been cast into the sea. No discipleship of Love is of much value that is not capable of following Rosaline's advice to Berowne[2] and spending a twelvemonth in a hospital—among the diseased, the maimed, the blind, creatures who have fallen upon the rock of Love and been broken. He must contemplate in close neighbourhood the streets and the Lock Hospitals[3] of London. It is the Principle which (outraged, no doubt, and perverted) has produced this with which the sentimental lover is proposing to play; the Principle which did not deny the possibility, even at the utmost end, of the lover falling into damnation and hell. God, on

1. See John 1:9.
2. See William Shakespeare, *Love's Labour's Lost*, act 5, scene 2, lines 836-50.
3. Hospitals for the treatment of venereal diseases.

50

the heights of mystical contemplation, has been seen by some, to make a plaything of humanity; it is a dangerous thing for humanity in the hitherward valley to make a plaything of its God. The Pythoness in Coventry Patmore's Ode saw in the depths of heaven "three butterflies at play",[4] but he who talked with her had himself been a Titan forging thunderbolts and had himself been all-but-blasted by the thunderbolts of Zeus.

Against this double danger, of ingenuity and sentimentality, the safeguard is alike two-fold. It is scepticism and devotion. That these two cannot always work together must, alas! be admitted. The entire *dévot*, the entire agnostic, each tend to be scornful of the other. But for those natures who are capable of wholly becoming one or the other, this does not much matter; such misunderstanding scorn is a small price to pay for the great gift of absolute surrender. It is more normal, however, for even the student of Romantic Theology, even in the relations with his or her lover, let alone the relations with Love, to desire to keep back something of the price. So long as this desire is felt to exist, so long, that is, as the lover is terribly conscious of his own self-will (even when it masquerades as self-denial) existing with a defiant inertia within him, so long he will be advised to pray for a double gift of the sceptical spirit. He may very well pray "Lord, I believe: help thou mine unbelief",[5] and leave it to God to deal with the ambiguity as seems fit. It is in an atmosphere warmed by the ardent sun of devotion, but drenched also by the cool rains of scepticism, at their proper periods, that the best crops are grown.

Such a combination is, in effect, not rarely experienced in love, though it is apt to be despised in religion. Many a lover knows that sudden sense of the mind protesting in mere delight and gay rebellious disbelief against the very presence of his lady. It is in a sense emotional rather than intellectual, though it expresses itself by intellectual as well as emotional reactions. It is a necessary element in wonder, and wonder (though perhaps subdued wonder) is an element in marriage, even after many years.

4. Coventry Patmore, *The Unknown Eros*, book II, number XIII, "De Natura Deorum," line 161. The line should read: "the fair butterflies at lovesome play."
5. Mark 9:24.

The other danger to which reference has been made, infidelity, is a danger common to all love; and though it has not, in this particular aspect, a greater moral guilt than in others, it has perhaps greater dangers about it. Since vision, or even belief, does not *per se* convey passion, not anyhow until it has been absorbed into the whole personality and become the controlling force of the individual life, it would be unfair to suppose that life to be held to a stricter judgement than its peers. The judgement indeed is stricter in one, and a very real, sense, but this sense is an inevitable part of the whole thesis. Infidelity to love consists in the deliberate preference of some other meaner motive and occupation to love, and the identification of love in marriage with Christ involves something very like the identification of infidelity with Antichrist. States of vision and belief change in a moment into their opposite; it was, as has often been seen, by the gates of the Celestial City that there was a path into hell.[6] The opposite of love is here something more than the dormant dislike which appears to be a normal part of a man's relations with his fellows, his friends, and his lover. It is much nearer positive hate, so near in its existence to love that it is capable of occupying in a moment the very seat of love, of centring everything else round it, as love does, and of extending itself to all other things and persons as love should do. Such a hate is not necessarily active, nor desires to avenge itself upon the person of the Beloved. It may, and no doubt sometimes does, carry sadism along with it, but it is no more sadism in itself than love is merely desire. It is a state of contemplation, holding itself in its place, so to speak, by an exercise of repulsion from instead of attraction to others. It is the Prince of the North in a house of eternal ice, as Dante saw him,[7] rooted and motionless in the intensity of his refusal, and lit only with the occasional gleam of a cold and unused malignity.[8]

If it were possible for man—as it may be—entirely to reach this state, it would be true of love as of religion that there is a state in which forgiveness is impossible to man; and Romantic Theology at any rate

6. See the conclusion of John Bunyan's *The Pilgrim's Progress*, Part 1.
7. *The Divine Comedy, Inferno*, canto XXXIV.
8. A new paragraph now begins in the MS (which I have followed), though not in the typescript.

would not shrink from such a deduction. It does not seem that the safeguard against either the lesser or the greater evil lies so much in scepticism as in the ardent and devoted heart, and (if this seems to be killed by the overwhelming presence of hatred) by the exercise of faith.

The gift of faith indeed is in Romantic as in other theology one of the accompaniments of the presence of Christ. In small things, in moments of boredom or dislike, this faith is capable of relieving the strain on the lovers by referring them to the Love they serve. These moments are felt to be, not opposed to, but a part of the divine power that binds them together, and as an explorer may find pleasure in some dangerous passage, so the lovers may observe with delighted interest the dull and uninteresting appearance of whoever was but lately the perfect embodiment of grace. "This also is He."[9] Responsibility is gone, and in its place there arises a quiet repose.

But if in small trials this faith is the safeguard, it is the only sort of protection against the greater danger. "Whosoever believeth in Me, though he were dead, yet shall he live: and whosoever liveth and believeth in Me shall never die."[10] To the lover caught in this second death, so much more terrible because so much more desirable than the mere collapse of love, such a sentence is his only hope. The collapse of love is the loss of the Christhood, but this second death is almost the Christhood itself transfigured into an infernal opposite of itself. Even here, made one with this ape of divinity, the lover, if he can do nothing else, can affirm against all emotion, all evidence, all desire, that these devils also can be cast out.

A minor peril, a peril of speculation and only indirectly of prac-

9. Not identified. Later, Williams often used the extended aphorism, "This also is Thou; neither is this Thou." He always denied having invented it and at one time attributed it, apparently wrongly, to St. Augustine. Its origin has not to my knowledge been found. Dr. Brian Horne, however, has noted its resemblance to phrases used in the Hindu Upanishads. This is especially so when in the Brihadaranyaka Upanishad the sage, speaking of the Soul (*Atman*), used the phrase "That Soul (*Atman*) is not this, it is not that (*neti, neti*)" (IV.v.15).

In the quotation above, Williams may have intended to write "Thou" instead of "He." Alternatively, it may suggest a different origin for what was later to be extended into his aphorism. We may also note the phrases in his poem "Counsels of Perfection" in *Windows of Night* (1925): "Nought save God can be" and "These too are He!"

10. See John 11:25-26.

tice—a disadvantage rather than a danger—lies in a certain tendency to transmute all discussion into terms of sex rather than to transmute the terms of sex into something else. The romantic who sees sex as a manifestation of God is in certain risk of talking of God as if he himself were in some way sexual. Doubtless in that supreme Simplicity which is God there is something to which our sex divisions correspond. But it is exceedingly dangerous to begin, unless after a long training in abstract thought, to begin speaking of the Masculine and Feminine principles in His Transcendence. It was not without reason that the Church has avoided the introduction of any such imagery into her doctrine of the Blessed Trinity. There is of course nothing absolutely wrong about it, though a certain risk of heresy, but it is apt to result in spreading a kind of slime over the highest levels of abstract ideas possible to men. In the end there is of course no abstraction, no principle of Justice or Fortitude or Temperance, apart from (whatever we mean by) the Personality of God. But this method of thought and speech is as it were a purification of the earthly mind. So, before any such metaphors are applied to the Divine Existence, the student should come to think of the sexes as merely manifestations in one current of energy of opposed and complementary *ideas*, in a world of which mathematics provides the only satisfactory symbol in the entire unemotionalism of its figures. When he has trained himself to regard all sexual questions, and indeed the whole created universe, as a series of equations, of which the true working will give him the value of x (x being love), he may proceed to consider x, in thought as well as devotion, as entire and perfect Being, as Love. It is the old trouble of the substitution of the lesser for the greater; it is not on the lower levels that one should, even with the best intentions, dally with the images of promiscuity in Deity.

Doctors and Documents*

The suggestion made in an earlier section of this pamphlet that it is a schematization of its subject—and perhaps to be rejected by the Church for that reason—more definite than has hitherto appeared is not to be read as putting in a claim on its behalf for equality with such notes of experience as have been left by the great masters of the science. Of these masters the first, for the Christian West, is Dante. He is the spring of all modern love literature; on the flood of the mighty river which had its source in him float all the strong silent men, all the sugary heroines, all the innocent or guilty couples, all the natural or perverted lovers, from that time to this. The feuilletons of the *Daily Mail* were already prophesied in the stars at the moment when Dante, wandering one day through Florence, suddenly stopped, overwhelmed and bewildered by the sight of Beatrice. The account of it, the first supreme offering of his adoration to Love by a great Catholic poet, is in the *Vita Nuova*, dated about 1294, and its complement and crown is in the *Divina Commedia* of about 1320. In the first Dante, after seeing Beatrice, beholds in a vision Love as "a lord of terrible aspect"; in the second she leads him through heaven till she gives him into the care of Saint Bernard and herself resumes her place in that Beatific Rose at whose heart is "the Love that moves the sun and all the stars".[1] And though there is not any definite proposal of Beatrice as

* There are certain books which, though extraordinarily valuable to the student, are not included in the present brief survey because they are not part of historic Christian thought; of such are the *Banquet* and the *Phaedrus* of Plato, and the *Zohar* of mediaeval Jewry. [Textual note by Williams]

1. The last line of *The Divine Comedy* (*Paradise*, canto XXXIII, line 145), in translation.

in this sense the sister and mirror of the Blessed Virgin, nor of the identity of these two names of Love, yet it is certain that the genius of Dante first showed us what may be called the religious spirit in Love. By the writings of Dante and of minds like his the rest of us have been made aware of the profundities which are concealed in this fastidious and passionate devotion; for phrases which might be used, as it were colloquially, by any lover, take on a sudden significance when used by these men, and we become aware that we do not excusably exaggerate in saying, for example, "It's heaven to be with her", but on the contrary express without perhaps realising it an eternal and immortal truth.

Unless the intensity of these records be felt by the reader, and their illumination perceived, they will nevertheless be regarded as nothing but exaggeration. And because literature depends so largely on the personal response by the reader, it cannot very well be held to prove anything in itself. No more than the Gospels prove the Deity of Christ does the work of these great lovers prove the theology of romantic love. But it corroborates, as the Gospels do, the hypothesis of the Church— corroborates it certainly to the Church alone, since to others it must appear part of that very hypothesis. To the non-romantic, as to the non-Christian, these documents are themselves part of that which they are sometimes rashly supposed to prove. It is for this reason that the Christian Church has been driven to define faith as being the direct gift of God; or, in other words, a non-rational assumption on the part of the believer. But since that Church has accepted as witnesses the records of those who lived with Christ, so it may accept also as witnesses the records of those who have lived with Love.

On the hypothesis of this identification of Christ and Love, the old dispute whether Beatrice was a woman or Theology loses a good deal of its importance. In a sense, the Blessed Virgin is herself the Theology of the Church—the Seat of Wisdom. In the same way Beatrice was herself Romantic Theology, for Dante, and (as his guide and patron) in a degree for all later lovers. The Invocation of Saints will apply to her and to Dante, and to other holy lovers and poets; although of course, since, on the hypothesis, each lover has his own living Theology, the saints of love are remoter from his needs than the saints of religion. But it is a heavenly courtesy, and an appreciation of the unity of the Church Romantic, so to invoke and adore them.

If we turn to the *Vita Nuova* itself, we shall find that it contains a few phrases of importance for the consideration of the subject; although, as was previously said, we shall find in this and the other documents to be mentioned rather notes made by the explorers of this mystical way than any scheme of defined intellectual study. And the first to be offered is the conclusion of a poem which has, it seems, puzzled the commentators, but on this interpretation is not so difficult. Dante has heard of the death of a lady who was often in the company of Beatrice, and has written two sonnets upon her. "I conceived," he says, "to say somewhat of her death, in guerdon of having seen her somewhile with my lady; which thing I spake of in the latter end of the verses that I writ in this manner, as he will discern who understands."[2] The latter end spoken of is the following stanza—

Whom now I mourn, no man shall learn from me
Save by the measure of these praises given.
Whoso deserves not Heaven
May never hope to have her company.

Where is the allusion to Beatrice here? That there must be one Dante has indicated; but the exact reference seems to have been a difficulty. Yet if Heaven is taken to *mean* Beatrice, there is no difficulty at all. This lady had often been in the company of Beatrice, and no-one therefore who did not deserve that company, which is Heaven, could hope to have her own fellowship.

A later poem speaks in similar terms, or even higher. Dante has determined to take for his writings "the theme of this most gracious being", but it seemed to him far too lofty a theme, unless he addressed the poem to other ladies of high birth and fair behaviour. The poem tells how the angels and saints pray to God that Beatrice may join them in heaven— "Heaven requireth Nought saving her". But God answers that she is to remain on earth yet awhile, for on earth is one who dreads the loss of her,

. . . Who in Hell unto the doomed shall say,
'I have looked on that for which God's chosen pray.'[3]

2. If "matter" is substituted for Williams's "manner" (probably a mistake in copying) he seems to be using the translation by Dante Gabriel Rossetti.
3. *Vita Nuova*. The lines are taken from the poem beginning: "Ladies that have intelligence in love." Williams is again using the translation by Rossetti.

Such a phrase as this compels us either to believe that Dante was speaking in all sincerity and concealed in this line a high and awful meaning, or to suppose that he was merely exaggerating. No-one who cares at all for the supreme poets, and especially for those who can least be accused of sentimentality, in virtue of their agonised hearts and tormented minds, their contemplation of the world's distress and refusal of easy comfort,—no-one who cares for them will be willing to believe in the second possibility. But if the first is true, if Dante really meant something by his "I have looked on that for which God's chosen pray", what can it be but that "which many prophets and mighty men desired to see and were not able"? It is fitting then, and then alone, that—as he records—he should in his own chamber "have prayed to the Blessed Virgin and said also 'O Love, aid thou thy servant'", before he "went suddenly to sleep like a beaten, sobbing child."

There are other matters upon which we might delay but it is necessary to refer briefly to other documents. The next that should be mentioned is the classical work in English literature upon a very great subject: viz., the *Morte D'Arthur.*[4] This of course is concerned chiefly with "the matter of Britain" but also with the mass of poetry and legend concerning the Graal. It would require a specialist to deal adequately with the Graal literature and with its possible relations to sex and love; here it must be sufficient to consider it as we have it in Malory's book. Whether Malory himself realised the significance of his 'novel' may be doubted; either hypothesis—that he was ignorant of its implications or that he deliberately suppressed them and made certain substitutions, is feasible. The bearing of the story on our present subject is rather indirect than direct, but to that extent it is certainly present. The achievement of the Graal Quest by Galahad takes place at a Mass sung in Sarras by "a man surrounded by angels" who sings "a Mass of our Lady". He

---

4. "A prose translation made from the French by Malory, in twenty-one books, and finished between Mar. 1469 and Mar. 1470. It was printed by Caxton in 1485. . . . The work is a skilful selection and blending of materials taken from the mass of Arthurian legends. The central story consists of two main elements: the reign of King Arthur ending in catastrophe and the dissolution of the Round Table; and the quest of the Holy Grail, in which Launcelot fails by reason of his sin, and Galahad succeeds." (Sir Paul Harvey, *Oxford Companion to English Literature*, 2d ed. [Oxford: Clarendon Press, 1940], p. 538).

declares himself to be Joseph of Arimathea, but that (in view of the immense respect paid to the story of the Graal) seems a little unsatisfactory, and it may be—with all humility—suggested that the real Celebrant is here Christ himself, who has already appeared to the chosen knights at the Castle of the Wounded King. That Galahad should be assumed into Divinity in his communion at a Mass of our Lady sung by Love using the Graal for vessel is a high close to the story. But it is not only the achievement itself nor even the questers which are noteworthy. The second of these, it will be remembered, was Percivale, who has some curious and rather obscure connection with Love. The dead body of his 'sister' accompanies the knights. Now there is no particular suggestiveness in a sister accompanying a brother; but if the 'sister' were the lady whom Percivale loves, not mortally, but in the high companionship of the Graal, as virgin loves virgin—then the presence of her 'dead body' is significant. The third quester is Bors, who is married and has two children. On this interpretation Galahad, Percivale, and Bors express the three degrees of love—love in marriage, love between two persons who are in contemplation of, but without desire for, each other, their desire being only towards God, and love whose contemplation and desire is alike towards nothing but God.

The birth of Galahad as given in the *Morte D'Arthur* also deserves attention. He is, in a certain sense, a son of enchantment, for he is the son of Lancelot and Elaine, the daughter of the Wounded King. But Lancelot on the night when Galahad was conceived was so wrought upon by spells that he supposed Elaine to be Queen Guinevere herself, else he would have had nothing to do with her, "for when was Lancelot wanderingly lewd?" The love between Lancelot and Guinevere is an inevitable and tragic love (as the love between any Christian man and woman may be said to be, on the hypothesis of Romantic Theology). But they are the greatest knight and the fairest woman in the world, and therefore in a sense archetypal lovers. Yet it is not from such a love that Galahad can be directly born, since even love is here of the nature of sin. But Lancelot is so moved by the enchantments of the Wounded King that he, in full sincerity of love and passionately honourable, does yet conceive upon the holy and predestined mother the predestined master of the Graal Quest. His devotion and toil and agony are not without their reward, and it is at the very moment of achievement that

Galahad, so conceived, and brought up through his childhood in a Convent of White Nuns, says to Sir Bors (the married knight), "Salute me to my lord, Sir Launcelot, my father, and as soon as ye see him, bid him remember of this unstable world." And after the death of Arthur and the dissolution of Camelot, the purpose of its building being achieved in Sarras, "Sir Launcelot took the habit of priesthood and a twelvemonth he sang mass". And when he died "he lay as if he smiled, and the sweetest savour about him that ever they felt". Such is the ending of the knight who in the "truest and the holiest story that is in this world" was "the truest lover of a sinful man that ever loved woman".

The child born of this lover is seen to be Galahad, and the whole purpose of Galahad is the Achievement of the Graal, the being made one with the Body and Blood of Love. This is brought about at the Mass sung by Love in the spiritual city—a Mass of our Lady, she who is herself historically Galahad and herself the Graal in which the Divine Body dwelt. This achievement of the Graal is looked forward to far away at the beginning of the *Morte D'Arthur*, where Balin smote the Dolorous Stroke with the spear that had pierced the side of Christ, and brought confusion on the land of Logres, and afterwards slew and was slain by his brother Balan. If this evil adventure were taken to be a parallel story with that of the Fall of Man, the misuse of sacred things and afterwards a fratricidal conflict between men, then it is significant that Merlin, who buries the brothers, prophesies that "there shall never man handle [Balin's] sword but the best knight of the world and that shall be Sir Launcelot or Galahad his son." In fact the curse still rests upon the sword when Launcelot holds it for he slays with it, during the civil troubles arising out of his love for Guinevere, "the man he loved best in all the world, Sir Gawaine". But the Wounded King is healed by Galahad; Arthur passes into mystery—being perhaps only another manifestation of that same royalty, and reassumed into it by his own wound in the Last Battle and the healing of the Archetypal wound. And Launcelot the great lover, in his year's singing of the Mass, is a servant and priest of the Mystery into which his son has already passed.

The story is a story, and must be read as such; it is not the connotations of a mystic nor the definitions of a theologian. But it is the supreme invention in Christendom of a story concerned with the adventures and ineffable destiny of romantic love.

We come in the next place to the work of a poet who may stand for the first example in English of what we called Dante—the religious mind in love and brooding over its experience; viz. John Donne, Dean of St. Paul's. Donne's work is perhaps remarkable rather for its poetic effectiveness and for its union of the ordinary religious language with love than for its familiarity with the high places of Romantic Theology. He is the lyric writer, the singer, as Malory is the novelist, and Dante the mystical philosopher. But he is (besides his own personal contribution) an example of a kind of poetry of which England possesses a fair amount, namely, love-poetry expressing itself in a religious vocabulary. It would not do to press the value of this too far; but it has a curious satisfaction of its own, and especially to the student of Romantic Theology. On the borderland between ordinary love-poetry and religious love-poetry lie such verses as Herrick's *To Anthea*:

> Now is the time when all the lights wax dim
> And thou, Anthea, must withdraw from him
> Who is thy servant: Dearest, bury me
> Under some holy oak or Gospel tree,
> Where though thou seest not thou mayst think upon
> Me yearly when thou goest procession.[5]

This has certainly no philosophical value, but its poetic value to the Romantic Theologian is not inconsiderable. It is the lights and incense of the Mass—not the Mass, nor even the Canon of the Mass.

A similar example is Carew's *To my Inconstant Mistress*, of which Mrs. Meynell says that "the solemn vengeance of this poem has a strange tone—not unique, for it had sounded somewhere in mediaeval poetry in Italy—but in a dreadful sense divine". And indeed the whole imagery is so gathered from religion and so intense is the passion that controls and directs it that the lofty judgement of the last line—

5. Robert Herrick, *To Anthea*, lines 1-6. The lines should read:

> Now is the time, when all the lights wax dim;
> And thou (*Anthea*) must withdraw from him
> Who was thy servant. Dearest, bury me
> Under that *Holy-oke*, or *Gospel-tree*:
> Where (though thou see'st not) thou may'st think upon
> Me, when thou yeerly go'st Procession.

61

> "Thou shalt be
> Damned for thy false apostacy"[6]—

has in it something more than the mere complaint of the deserted lover.

To this kind of verse Donne himself contributed some of the most striking poems. Such is the *Funeral*, in which he bids "whoever comes to shroud him not to touch that subtle wreath of hair which crowns my arm", for

> 'tis my outward soul,
> Viceroy to that, which unto heaven being gone,
> Will leave this to control
> And keep these limbs, her provinces, from dissolution."[7]

But perhaps the poems in which the religious sense of love is most felt—indirectly but definitely—are those in which he speaks obscurely of some hidden manner of love, *Negative Love, The Undertaking, The Relic,* and a part of *The Ecstasy*.

> First, we loved well and faithfully,
> Yet knew not what we loved, nor why;
> Difference of sex we never knew
> No more than guardian angels do;
> Coming and going, we
> Perchance might kiss, but not betwixt those meals.[8]

Or again:

> If that be simply perfectest
> Which can by no way be express'd
> But negatives, my love is so.
> To all, which all love, I say no.[9]

---

6. Thomas Carew, *To My Inconstant Mistress*, lines 14-15.
7. *The Funeral*, stanza 1. Williams slightly paraphrases the first three lines of the stanza.
8. *The Relic*, lines 23-28. Lines 25 and 26 should read:

> Difference of sex no more we knew,
> Than our guardian angels do.

9. *Negative Love*, lines 10-12.

Or again:

> If, as I have, you also do,
> Virtue attir'd in woman see,
> And dare love that, and say so too,
> And forget the He and She.
>
> And if this love, though placéd so,
> From profane men you hide,
> Which will no faith on this bestow,
> Or, if they do, deride;
>
> Then you have done a braver thing
> Than all the Worthies did;
> And a braver thence will spring,
> Which is, to keep that hid.[10]

If this is not an approach to the love of Love himself, it seems to mean nothing at all. The protest against, and reply to, it is given in *The Ecstasy*, where the senses are praised for their due worth in being the functions of the soul and assisting it to its proper knowledge of itself. That Donne wrote many poems scoffing at love and faithfulness is to say no more than that he was not one of Love's saints but one of his poets. He complains, he rebels, he defies, but he rises again and again into the contemplation of this high state. "O 'tis imposture all," he cries in *Love's Alchemy*, of the "hidden mystery", the "centric happiness" of love;[11] but in the end he knows that "all divinity Is love or wisdom".[12]

---

10. *The Undertaking*, stanzas 5-7.

11. *Love's Alchemy*, lines 1-6; these lines read in full:

> Some that have deeper digged love's mine than I,
> Say where his centric happiness doth lie;
> I have loved, and got, and told,
> But should I love, get, tell, till I were old,
> I should not find that hidden mystery;
> O, 'tis imposture all.

12. *A Valediction of the Book*, lines 28-29. Note that Williams wrote "wisdom" by mistake for "wonder." Thus the lines should read:

> since all Divinity
> Is love or wonder.

This divinity Donne did not profess as a theology; he felt it sometimes as a religion. Something of the same sort is true of the greatest of English religious love-poets, Coventry Patmore; but only so much as serves to insist upon the intensity of Patmore's spiritual experience of that religion. No later commentator upon Romantic Theology but must continually feel how unnecessary his work is when he considers the many profound maxims which lie in the work of that great poet and mystic. Yet the mystics may sometimes leave it to infinitely lesser men to define or enunciate the dogmas of their experience; so that, although a couplet or a sentence or a line may contain infinitely more than (for example) this essay, yet the essay is not perhaps entirely superfluous as a direction. Patmore himself claimed to be the first to praise marriage as the root of all our love to man and God. Unfortunately the experience of most of his readers in this other kind of love is usually so limited that to them "all our love to man and God" sounds a much less important affair than the "nuptial love" with which Patmore began. Religious belief does not matter in reading poetry, but a sense of mythology does, and it is a matter of regret that our sense of mythology should have become so exhausted as to prevent most modern readers from receiving any enlargement of emotion from the word "God". So far as he touched upon our side of the subject Patmore tended to regard it as a symbolism rather than as theology, and romantic love to be rather symbolised by Saint John the Baptist than identified with Christ.* In so far as this love is but the herald of religious love for God, in so far as the Divine Principle absorbs into Himself all human functions and intentions, and will be content with nothing but a willingness to be divorced from everything and everyone but Himself, this is a true and necessary doctrine. The whole of Patmore's work in prose and verse is a record of this process, a record too dreadful and intimate to be discussed. To speak of the later Odes, nay even to read them, seems sometimes almost like eavesdropping at

---

* In fairness it should be added that this interpretation seems to be supported by the Last Gospel at the Mass, used in all Roman and many Anglican churches. John "is not that Light but is sent to bear witness of that light" [John 1:8—ED. NOTE]. In the thesis of Romantic Theology, John would be the greatest teacher—in life or in books—whom the lover had known before the coming of Love. But it is not altogether a satisfactory reference. [Textual note by Williams]

a saint's prayers; even for a disciple of the saint there is something unbecoming in it, for the detached and sceptical neighbour it is a breach of those manners which are the foundation of all morality. And sometimes to the saint the definition of the laws which govern his movements in that world which is Christ would seem an equal breach of courtesy. Many of those laws Patmore declared in "bitter, sweet, few and veiled"[13] poems, but he hinted only at the full identification of love and Christ.

It would be useless to attempt a summary or analysis of his work beyond this. It is for the greater mystics even among love-mystics. "First the natural; afterwards the supernatural",[14] he said; the one question that remains, after him, to be decided finally by the Church is whether, in the end, even that division can be, save for purposes of morality, maintained. He certainly would have been the first to maintain the continuity of all love. "God's grace is the only grace, and all grace is the grace of God";[15] "I loved her for the sake of God, and for the ray she was of Him";[16] "Him loved I reverently as Cause, Her sweetly as Occasion of all good",[17] and so on. And all definition, all schematization, would be but vain labour if it took away from this close sense of God and the Beloved. It is only because definitions and schemes are for many of us, lesser minds and lesser souls, the divine nurses of divine things that any further note has here been attempted. By some such definition a wise pagan—who accepts love but not religion, or religion but not love—or a devout Mahommedan—who believes in both but as separate, almost irreconcilable things—may perhaps incline to believe that there is a credible answer to one of the supreme questions of the world—

13. Coventry Patmore, The Unknown Eros, book II, number XII, "Eros and Psyche," line 203.

14. Patmore, The Rod, the Root and the Flower, 2d rev. ed. (London: G. Bell & Sons, 1911), p. 9. The original reads: "The natural first, afterwards the supernatural."

15. Patmore, The Angel in the House, book I, canto X, prelude 1.

16. The Angel in the House, book I, canto X, stanza 4. The line should read "I loved her in the name of God" rather than "I loved her for the sake of God."

17. Patmore, Amelia, lines 87-88. The lines should read:

And I, of Him loved reverently, as Cause,
Her sweetly, as Occasion of all good.

65

What in its ruddy orbit lifts the blood,
Like a perturbed moon of Uranus,
Reaching to some great world in ungauged darkness hid?[18]

With Patmore should be reckoned another document which has been the cause of some heart-burning: *The Song of Songs which is Solomon's*. Between the devout minds who insist that this book is nothing but a parable and the critical who insist that it is nothing of a parable, *the Song of Songs* has fared badly. The Church, having by Divine inspiration included it in the Canon, has felt uneasy about it ever since, just as she has felt uneasy about marriage. Of book and sacrament alike she has protested that they signify the marriage of Christ and the Church and has not allowed herself to insist upon the manner and value of the symbolism. The intense passion of the *Song* is a mortal passion moving and sustained by an immortal principle: it needs for its full perfection just the identification of Christ and Love which this theology proposes. Nor is there any need to distinguish carefully whether it is Love or the mortal lover of whom the daughters of Jerusalem ask "What is thy beloved more than another beloved, O thou fairest among women? what is thy beloved more than another beloved, that thou dost so charge us?"[19] It is in the certitude of the union of love that the Shulamite answers, beholding her beloved glorious with all the graces of Christ, "My beloved is white and ruddy, the chiefest among ten thousand. . . . His mouth is most sweet: yea, he is altogether lovely. This is my beloved and this is my friend, O daughters of Jerusalem."[20]

18. Patmore, *The Unknown Eros*, book II, number I, "To the Unknown Eros," lines 33-35.
19. Song of Solomon 5:9.
20. Song of Solomon 5:10, 16.

CHAPTER VII

Other Aspects of Romantic Theology

It was said in the second section that, though this essay was devoted to a study of Romantic Theology in reference to marriage, yet that its principles are true in relation to other romantic occupations of man; and it seems worth while to indicate here very briefly one or two of the most important.

And first a word must be said on that aspect of love which was referred to in the last section under the names of Donne and Sir Percivale. There appears to be a mode of romantic love felt by some and perhaps followed by a few minds which finds its vocation in the virginal life. This does not include the celibate as such; he—on the hypothesis—is called to follow God directly and not by the indirect method of marriage, and this business has been dealt with in many books under the heading of Mystical Theology. A very interesting parallel could be drawn between mysticism, with its illumination, its dark nights, its purgation, its union, and marriage. The parallel is not developed here for fear of confusing the issue; Romantic Theology must stand or fall on its own claims, independent of the help of its lofty sisters. But if the Church ever considers the problem of marriage seriously Romantic and Mystical Theology will find themselves closely akin.

Virginal love is that which, arising normally between a man and a woman, finds its method in the rejection rather than the acceptance of the ordinary physical approach. It is not, in this sense, particularly *ascetic*; that is, it does not, deliberately and warring against itself, set aside the graces and gifts of the body: it may rather be defined as that kind of love which is so occupied with contemplation that it has no room for desire. Other and worser emotions may imitate it, so easily deceived is man: fear and (again) sentimentality may easily pretend to its beauty. For this reason it seems desirable that a certain asceticism in other things should accompany virginal love, but they are not the same thing. The poets have taught us, rightly, that the first instinct of nearly all love is towards virginity:

> "the rash oath of virginity
> Which is first love's first cry."[1]

> "I would give all the world that she should love me,
> My soul that she should never learn to love."[2]

> "O soul, knock softly lest she hear,
> Knock softly, lest her hands undo the door."[3]

It seems therefore to be a normal emotion, and probably might be, and possibly is, more commonly practised than appears. And as the courtesies of marriage, touch and kiss and caress, are loved for their own sake, so the refusals of virginity should be. They are the means by which Love in them makes itself manifest.

In those lives where virginity rules it seems probable that the presence of the Divine Principle is more swiftly and more continuously recognised than in lives of marriage. The end is of course the same—the growing to "the stature of the fulness of Christ".[4]

Another means by which Christ lives is in friendship. Friendship is to marriage, say, as Saint Thomas, the Angel of the Schools, is to the Blessed Virgin. It lacks, and must lack at all events while conception and birth are by means of the woman, complete manifestation in the physical world. The joy felt in the physical presence of a friend is a curiously variable quantity; with some it is hardly present at all, with others, it is almost the chief thing. But in any case, though the Divine Presence is there in contemplation it is not there in corporeal desire and

---

1. Coventry Patmore, *The Unknown Eros*, book I, number I, "Saint Valentine's Day," lines 9-10.
2. Not identified.
3. A quotation from Charles Williams's own poem, "Of Diffidence in Love", sonnet 36 in *The Silver Stair*, 1912.
4. Ephesians 4:13.

fruition. It is productive, as the Divine Presence must always be, but rather on the intellectual than the physical plane. In its degree the process of friendship between any two individuals is a process of marriage, and in this connexion one of them has often been said to be 'feminine' to the other's masculine. But in truth this parallel between the corporeal intercourse of lovers and the mental intercourse of friends is hardly stable. For two friends in any hour's companionship are each of them both masculine and feminine; both give, both receive; now one dominates, now the other. It is a republican and not a hierarchical relationship taken as a whole, though the position of the two at any one moment may be hierarchical.

Besides this, friendship is often a state which includes more than two. It is a group-state, corresponding with and opening upon, both in width and intensity, the secular rather than the religious world. To the individual, friendship is a means of egress upon the whole world of mankind as love is a means of egress upon God. The lover who, most happy, has also his group of friends, is thus a partaker in the Commonwealth and the Church. And as the Church would (it is believed) gain considerably by a realisation of the communion with itself which is to be found in romantic love, so on the other hand it may be by the establishment and interaction of groups of friends over the whole world that our social and international troubles may eventually be solved. Such a solution is, no doubt, far enough away, since it involves on the part of the individual not only activity in friendship on his own part but an ardent belief in those other groups of which he is not a part. But this belief, together with a belief in the Deity of romantic love—"a free Church in a free State"[5]—promises a happier internationalism than we have hitherto foreseen.*

Neither of these correspondences is of course exclusive. There is friendship in love, as there is love in friendship; neither the delighted

5. The Italian statesman Cavour spoke in 1861 of "this great principle: a free church in a free state" ("questo gran principio: Libera Chiesa in libero Stato").

* But the basis of all politics, all social reform, all revolution, is in the parable of the sheep and the goats [Matthew 25:31-46—ED. NOTE]. Not only in his universal manhood but as the Love of marriage is Christ naked and hungry, sick and in prison: and it is to clothe and feed, to heal and free him, and all his elect with him, that no two lovers shall be deprived of the possibilities of love by social injustice, that the activities of all fortunate lovers should be in some degree directed. [Textual note by Williams]

contemplation nor the moving desire of love exhaust its wonderful potentialities. There is a state, experienced most frequently in the most fortunate marriages, when contemplation and desire both repose in the peace and content of a subdued harmony. "I have not called you servants, but I have called you friends",[6] Love says to the lovers, though the friendship established and maintained in this particular manner of His life differs somewhat from other friendships; as any friendship based on a common spiritual experience will probably differ from any other, even the noblest, kind of friendship. It seems to be in the nature of romantic love to contain within itself the manner of all other kinds of love: the love of friends, the love of children, the love of mothers, are all rooted in this; not as aimed at their respective objects, friends or parents or children, but as exercised in those particular manners towards the other lover. This is another instance of the identification of romantic love with Christ.

Nevertheless, in a vaguer and less defined way, they exist also, it is to be supposed, in any relation of man into which the element of sincere and simple attraction enters. The term 'romantic love' has been used throughout to mean sexual love; but there are other manifestations of it—learning, art, sport, nature, politics, stamp-collecting. Of these we are generally willing to admit that love of learning, art, nature, perhaps politics, has something divine about it. We are not perhaps so willing to admit football or stamp-collecting. Yet it is difficult to see why the division should be made. If the astronomer is recognised as partaking in the Morning Joy with which the redeemed contemplate God in His Creation, may not the stamp-collector share it likewise? Any occupation exercising itself with passion, with self-oblivion, with devotion, towards an end other than itself, is a gateway to divine things. If a lover contemplating in rapture the face of his lady, or a girl listening in joy to the call of the beloved, are worshippers in the hidden temples of our Lord, is not also the spectator who contemplates in rapture a batsman's stroke or the collector gazing with veneration at a unique example of the Buenos Aires issue of 1895 (or whatever)? There are more dangers certainly in this vocation; of which not the least is the passivity of the thing admired. The stamp—in itself, and apart from the difficulties of

6. John 15:15.

procuring it—does not exercise any active influence on or antagonism to its owner. No wife or husband, however bemused or downtrodden, is probably ever quite so inactive, so entirely at her owner's disposal, as a stamp: and the danger of breaking the Second Commandment (as it was interpreted in the fourth section) and imposing a personal idea or emotion on the object beloved, the universe at large, and God its Creator, is increased to an almost infinite degree. Love for a stamp is far more like symbolism of than identification with Christ. Yet the possibilities are there: the way is longer and more dangerous—but here also He and none other is the Beginning and at long last the End.

It is because of the length of this way, rather than from any essential difference in kind, that love of nature, love of art, love of learning have been recognised as being of greater value than the rest. In all of these there is a certain 'opposition' in the object which, while making the love a more difficult task, makes it in its greatest practitioners more obviously holy. There is no doubt as intense a selfishness, as great a desire to own, in the normal lover of a woman, of nature, of music or poetry, or of 'the enclytic *de*'[7] as in the stamp-collector. But—to say nothing of the woman—there is on the whole more possibility of this selfishness being abolished, of this love rising into the "stature of the fullness of Christ",[8] so long as the love is sincere. Wandering in a country field on a Sunday evening is not love of nature; love of nature includes the tiger, the scorpion, the liver-fluke, and a belief that these things also are somehow part of a divine and supreme Whole. So with the others. There is not much danger of infidelity to a stamp; there is much danger of infidelity to a cobra. The measure of the

---

7. A rule of accentuation. The quotation is taken from Robert Browning's *A Grammarian's Funeral*:

> So, with the throttling hands of death at strife,
>   Ground he at grammar;
> Still, through the rattle, parts of speech were rife:
>   While he could stammar
> He settled *Hoti's* business—let it be!—
>   Properly based *Oun*—
> Gave us the doctrine of the enclitic *De*.
>   (lines 125-31)

8. Ephesians 4:13.

71

precipice is the measure of the height; but there are minds for whom the mere kerb of the pavement falls away into incredible abysses.

There is another test, but one almost impossible for men to make; and that is productiveness. "A God's embraces never are in vain."[9] But productiveness is of many kinds and cannot be discovered until all things are made known. Children are the most obvious example, and one sign of the essential divinity of marriage; ideas are another and serve a like office for friendship; but what secret and holy states of consciousness may not be brought into existence by what appears a useless and wandering love? Nor are these states of consciousness without influence on the whole world of mankind, any more than the secret devotions of a nun. The pure devotion of a philosopher or an explorer plays its part in the search for the most holy Graal. He who, not in any sense for himself or to himself, is surrendered to an entire ardour cannot be said to be far from the Kingdom which will manifest Itself at Its chosen time; the sooner if, as has been insisted throughout, this ardour is directed and controlled by the doctrines of the Christian Religion.

*   *   *

To the life of the Church, which is the life of Christ; to the illuminated mind of mankind, which is the mind of Christ, the thesis of this book must be submitted. The discussions of this last section are not an essential part of it. The thesis itself is that, and that only, which was formulated earlier—the identification of romantic love with Christ and of marriage with his life. No lesser word than identification will serve. Symbolism—strictly speaking—ought to serve; but the common rather careless use of the word suggests rather a remote likeness than the very Presence of the God—not manifested in his full glory, but more fully and more universally manifested than in any other manner; and containing within Himself all those potentialities which (in terms of time) are His, though they are eternally fulfilled in Act. The deduction from this thesis is that it has been inevitably left to the Church, who contains the secret of the Incarnation, the Passion, the Resurrection, to allow this identification to become known. It is her consciousness of this

9. Patmore, The Unknown Eros, book II, number XII, "Eros and Psyche," line 56.

which has caused her to speak as she has done of marriage; it is her unconsciousness of it that has hampered her in speaking of it. If in the end her mind, which is the mind of all mankind dwelling on divine things, should pronounce against this proposition, there will of course be no more to be said. But the Mind of the Church, like the mind of any lady her sister, is capable of strange statements before it speaks with that sudden rightness which her lovers know and adore.

If marriage is not Christ, it is either a morality or a natural phenomenon, expanding all this illumination, all those graces, merely for the sake of reproducing the race. But if it is, then indeed He is the light that lighteneth every man that cometh into the world,[10] then indeed our eyes have seen his salvation

"Which Thou hast prepared before the face of all people;
To be a light to lighten the Gentiles, and to be the glory of
Thy people Israel."[11]

10. John 1:9.
11. Luke 2:30-32. Williams is following the wording found in the Order for Evening Prayer in the Church of England's Book of Common Prayer rather than the Authorized Version of the Bible.

Sequel

Alice M. Hadfield

A few months before Charles Williams had written *Outlines of Romantic Theology*, the Oxford University Press had moved its offices a few hundred yards from Amen Corner to Amen House in Warwick Square, within the boundaries of the ancient City of London: indeed, a piece of Londinium's Roman wall could be seen in its basement.

A new librarian now appeared, the fair-haired, intelligent, vivid Phyllis Jones. Within months a new social and literary life engendered by this move to Amen House had raised up a Lady to epitomize it. Charles' life burst open into creating the *Masques*, plays in light verse about the work and personalities of the Press, and round them a flurry of light, amusing, joyful poetry. He was again in love.

She was not. Flattered at first to be the quiet center of Charles' cyclonic outpouring of love, the twenty-three year old had little interest in a man fifteen years her senior. Before long Charles realized he was rushing down a one-way street. Three years later, in 1927, she met the man she was later to marry; three years more, and Charles discovered that she had fallen in love with an older colleague of his at the Press; four years later again she left the firm.

We do not know, and cannot guess, what might have happened if she had returned his love. What did happen was a widening and deepening of his ideas on romantic theology, as he mentally straddled the problem of reconciling the old and new experiences—both true—of love. After about 1928 he ceased to be an occasional writer and became a real one. Words poured out of him in poetry, dramatic verse, novels, and literary criticism, and in these and in his letters we can trace what was going on within.

We get glimpses of Phyllis everywhere; glimpses too of the expanding universe of his thinking about love:

> Nor do I now in any wise hate the earth,
> Conception, and the growing of small things,
> As Hamlet did . . .   I . . .
> Have given my heart from its own spiny charge
> To the full circle of the rounded O'.[1]

Or, a little later:

> *Vincenzo:*   O believe
>   your happiness must be established.
>
> *The Duchess:*   How
>   established?
>
> *Vincenzo:*   By no other means than toil,
>   attention, adoration, practice of love.
>
>   .   .   .   .   .   .
>
> *Vincenzo:*   She once obeyed,
>   and her obedience ruins me for ever.
>   I would be somebody in heaven, and now
>   I am forever nothing and in hell,
>   Yet she obeyed! O to obey, to follow!
>   To follow to her and to follow her
>   are one; it is to be her, which I was
>   ere she became the Prince and I a devil.[2]

There is something of Phyllis in his analysis of Shakespeare's Cressida:

> There is a world where our mothers are unsoiled and Cressida is his; there is a world where our mothers are soiled and Cressida is given to Diomed. What connexion have those two worlds? "Nothing at all, unless that this were she."[3]

There is also something of her in the character Chloe in his novel *Many Dimensions*, published in 1931.

1. *A Myth of Shakespeare* (Oxford University Press, 1929), p. 142.
2. "The Chaste Wanton," in *Three Plays* (Oxford University Press, 1931), pp. 91, 124.
3. *The English Poetic Mind* (Russell & Russell, 1932), p. 60.

He was not offered the chance to be sexually unfaithful, so he used his eyes:

> I saw the hand of the queen Iseult;
> down her arm a ruddy bolt
> fired the tinder of my brain. . . .[4]

In 1934 Phyllis married and went to live in Java. He still loved her. But now, away from familiar London and the interesting, intense life of the Press, she began to feel lonely and strange both in her marriage and in her Eastern surroundings. So she began to lean on Charles, just when he was hoping for the strain to be eased. In this situation he discovered a new facet of romantic theology, something he could indeed do that would benefit her. He ends a letter: "And now, inseparable comrade, what do we do about substituted love? Might it be useful?"[5]

For Williams, romantic theology was never just a subject for a book but a lifelong way of daily living. On 4 July 1925, soon after *Outlines* had been written, in a very bad temper with his wife, his son, and his home life, he lets fly at them and marriage in a letter to Pellow; then ends, laughing at himself but also very seriously: "Everything in the above letter is to be understood according to the Mind of Christendom as defined by the principles of Romantic Theology."

In 1929 a young student of his, Thelma (now Shuttleworth), was in love and planning marriage. In one letter to her he suggests that she read the (Anglican) collect for Whitsunday and then continues: "All the collects have their application to romantic theology as well as dogmatic; from all of them the devout lover may extract instruction and aid." In another he says firmly: "Either our mortal love is to be believed as an epiphany and presence of the Divine Perfection, or it is not. And to accept it as such without doing something about it is sentimentality. . . . It may be the beginning of something (apart from human relations—however beautiful) which is at last to be the final end of the soul. But to find it that, we must believe on it and submit to it—whatever doom it brings. And

---

4. *Taliessin through Logres* (Oxford University Press, 1938), p. 34.
5. In my book *Charles Williams: An Exploration of His Life and Work* (New York: Oxford University Press, 1983), I describe substitution as a "compact to bear another's burden. One can take by love the worry of another, or hold a terror, as one member of Christ's life helping, through that life, another member in trouble" (p. 32n).

how terrible some of those dooms are only those who have endured them know." He sees the living out of romantic theology as lifelong. When Thelma tells him that she has been practicing it for nine months he replies: "Nine months—heavens, child, nine years and then some will find you still at the beginning. You are beginning infinity, you are learning eternity."

Throughout the course of his second love for Phyllis, he did not deny the validity of his first for Florence, though he came very near to it, as in this letter written to Phyllis in 1935:

> I should like to hear Romantic Theology declared and defended from the Throne of Augustine. The thesis was metaphysically formulated before the Celian Star rose, I reluctantly admit, but it was the full Celian sun that uttered to all of me the identical words of Christ: 'I am come that ye may have life, and that ye may have it more abundantly'. Which certainly was the gift Celia bestowed.[6]

That "reluctantly" is a near miss.

By that year he must have felt that he had reached rock-bottom. Nevertheless, he had maintained his marriage intact, though battered. For some years he seems to have spent most of his time at home writing, partly to get down on paper the flowering of his intellect, but partly also, I suspect, to avoid the silences, difficulties, intimacies of a relationship under strain. Yet in fact he had only reached the end of the beginning.

If we now re-read the first few pages of Chapter VI of *Outlines of Romantic Theology*, we shall again become aware of the special power that Dante and the *Morte d'Arthur* had upon Williams's thinking about romantic theology. From 1924 to the mid-1930s, he had chosen to investigate its tributaries rather than to plunge again into its main stream. But, about the time of the writing and production of his verse play *Thomas Cranmer of Canterbury* in 1936 in the great cathedral, something happened. Was there a recall of what he had said a year before—"I should like to hear Romantic Theology declared and defended from the Throne of Augustine"? For he now returned to those two influences upon the *Outlines*, which he had then so imperfectly understood. Thereafter a search for light thrown upon the operations

---

6. The "Throne of Augustine" = Canterbury Cathedral; "Celia" = Phyllis. This letter is quoted in full in my book *Charles Williams: An Exploration*, pp. 128-29.

of romantic love by the Arthurian myths and the writings of Dante was to be his life's main work.

Interest in the Arthurian stories went back to his youth. After 1924 a few of his poems on the subject were published; many more were written—notably a series called "The Coming of Arthur." None were quite successful. Then, in the mid-1930s, he began the series of Taliessin poems which were published in *Taliessin through Logres* (Oxford University Press, 1938) and *The Region of the Summer Stars* (Poetry [London] Editions, 1944), and which meant so much to him.[7]

We know that he had read and appreciated Dante before the *Outlines*. Afterwards, however, he wrote in such terms as this in *Shadows of Ecstasy* (published in 1933 by Victor Gollancz, but much of it written earlier):

> He had certainly heard of Dante and Beatrice, of Tristram and Iseult, of Lancelot and Guinevere, but there he stopped. He had hardly heard, he had certainly never brooded over, that strange identification of Beatrice with Theology and of Theology with Beatrice by which our great poet has justified centuries of else doubtful minds. (Pp. 57-8)

or this in 1930 to Thelma:

> Remember that Dante wrote of the *"New Life"* first, all about love, and then passed on to *"The Divine Comedy"*, which is about the Eternal Justice, but I don't mean merely being "just" to people. "I want to be just to her" is as useless a phrase as "I love her". Certainly Love and Justice are one, but one has to learn Love as Justice, and I do—I really do—believe that is at a later stage of life than Love as love.

He began again to study Dante, and especially to read the Italian. Happily, Italian is an easy language to follow, even if one has never learned it, given that one is well grounded in French and, like Williams, also in Latin.

The edition by E. Moore in the Oxford Dante was available, and in 1932 the Oxford University Press put into its World's Classics series another with parallel English and Italian texts, this time with an English translation by Melville Anderson into *terza rima*, corresponding to

7. For more information on these poems see chapter 9 in my book *Charles Williams: An Exploration.*

Dante's original. A third edition with parallel Italian text and prose translation had long been available in Dent's Temple Classics. When I knew Williams he constantly used the pocket volumes of the Temple Classics, but when he first quoted Italian in his next book, *He Came Down from Heaven*, he seems to be using Moore's text.

What previously he must have known in his mind, he now realized with his whole nature: the greatest European poet was writing about his own subject of romantic theology, and in words that could not fail to move him. Who could not be stirred by Beatrice's words:

> "Guardaci ben: ben sem, ben sem Beatrice.
> Come degnasti d'accedere al monte?
> non sapei tu che qui è l'uom felice?"

> "Look well: we are, we are indeed Beatrice.
> How is it you have deigned to draw near the mountain?
> Did you not know that here man is happy?"[8]

Filled with excitement, he coincidentally received an invitation from R. Ellis Roberts to contribute to a series of short books to be published by Heinemann under the general title of "I Believe: A Series of Personal Statements." *He Came Down from Heaven* appeared in 1938. Of its seven chapters, chapter 5 ("The Theology of Romantic Love"), chapter 6 ("The Practice of Substituted Love"), and chapter 7 ("The City") dealt with the working out of love. His experience with Phyllis Jones must have given him a basis for chapter 6, and the location of the Amen House offices of the Oxford University Press within the City of London must have contributed to chapter 7.

Chapter 5, his first substantial statement on romantic theology since the *Outlines* of fourteen years before, exhibits a great leap forward in his thinking, the ordering of his ideas, and his ability to express them.

Along with Dante, Shakespeare, and Milton, Wordsworth is now all-important to him, and he begins chapter 5 with a quotation from Wordsworth's *The Prelude*:

> There are in our existence spots of time,
> That with distinct pre-eminence retain

8. *The Divine Comedy, Purgatory*, canto XXX, lines 73-75.

SEQUEL

A renovating virtue, whence . . .
our minds
Are nourished and invisibly repaired.
(Book 12, lines 208-15)

Since Christ's time, he says, one change able to fill "men's pre-eminent moments with new nourishment and new repair" had "affected perhaps more than all the rest . . . the casual fancies and ordinary outlook of men and women" (p. 85). That change was the discovery of romantic love in eleventh-century Provence. Here he follows C. S. Lewis's *The Allegory of Love,* then recently published. (I myself doubt if it can be so dated, but that is not finally important.) Then, Williams goes on: "There entered into the relations between the sexes a philosophical, even a religious, idea" (p. 87).

He continues: "There is no accepted agreement upon what the state which our grandfathers used to call 'falling in love' involves. It is neither sex appetite pure and simple; nor, on the other hand, is it necessarily related to marriage. It is something like a state of adoration" (p. 88). As an illustration he quotes from another of his great poetical influences, Milton, words spoken by Adam about Eve:

> ". . . when I approach
> Her loveliness, so absolute she seems
> And in herself complete, so well to know
> Her own, that what she wills to do or say
> Seems wisest, virtuousest, discreetest, best.
> All higher knowledge in her presence falls
> Degraded; Wisdom in discourse with her
> Loses, discount'nanced, and like Folly shows;
> Authority and Reason on her wait,
> As one intended first, not after made
> Occasionally; and, to consummate all,
> Greatness of mind and nobleness their seat
> Build in her loveliest, and create an awe
> About her, as a guard angelic placed."
> (*Paradise Lost*, book 8, lines 546-59)

"This then," he says, "is the contemplation of the object of love from a state of romantic love. There has been and is, now as always,

80

only one question about this state of things: is it serious? is it capable of intellectual treatment? is it capable of belief, labour, fruition? is it (in some sense or other) *true? . . .* Can this state of things be treated as the first matter of a great experiment? . . . The end, of course, is known . . . : it is the establishment of a state of *caritas,* of pure love, the mode of expansion of one moment into eternity" (pp. 89-90).

At this point he begins a discussion of Dante, the range of whose whole work "provides a complete account of the making of the experiment and of its success" (p. 90). Its beginnings are told in *La Vita Nuova (The New Life).* Dante first saw Beatrice Portinari when she was nine, saw her several times more, and then, when she was eighteen, realized that he loved her; he wrote of her: "I say that when she appeared from any place, there was . . . no enemy remaining to me, but a flame of *caritas* possessed me, which made me pardon anyone who had offended me; and if anyone had then asked me concerning anything, my answer would have been only *Love,* with a face clothed in humility" (p. 99).

Beatrice died, and later Dante was to marry another woman. But the Beatrician experience remained true, and he continued to work at why it was true, and what it involved for him. In a later book, *Il Convivio (The Banquet),* Dante analyzed his experience of romantic love, and Williams summarizes this analysis (pp. 92-97). Later Beatrice's "nature is more particularly declared . . . in a very different kind of poem" (p. 102), *La Divina Commedia, The Divine Comedy.*[9] Dante finds himself in a savage wood. Thence Virgil escorts him through hell—visible knowledge of sins and their consequences—through purgatory, and finally to paradise. There Beatrice finds him, and he feels again *"d'antico amor . . . la gran potenza,"* the great power of the old love. "Here, surrounded by angels, prophets, evangelists, virtues, Romantic Love is seen to mirror the Humanity and Deity of the Redeemer." "But really," Williams goes on, "though he now imagined it more clearly and more strongly, he had not known anything different, in essence or in principle, when the face of the Florentine girl flashed her 'good morning' at him along the street of their City" (pp. 103-5).

Now comes Williams's link with Christianity.

9. Here, "Comedy" denotes a narrative poem with a happy ending.

It is possible to follow this method of love without introducing the name of God. But it is hardly possible to follow it without proposing and involving as an end a state of *caritas* of the utmost possible height and breadth, nor without allowing to matter a significance and power which (of all the religions and philosophies) only Christianity has affirmed.

If, however, we retain the name and idea of God, and if there is any common agreement about the state of exalted experience known as the state of "falling in love," then it is possible to go further and relate that experience to the Incarnation of the kingdom. When Messias said: "Behold my mother" he was, in this relation, merely accurate. The beloved (male or female) is seen in the light of a Paradisal knowledge and experience of good. Christ exists in the soul, in joy, in terror, in a miracle of newness. *Ecce, omnia nova facio.*[10] He who is the mystical child of the lovers sustains and supports them: they are the children of their child. "We speak that we do know and testify that we have seen. . . . No man hath ascended up into heaven, but he that came down from heaven, even the Son of Man which is in heaven." (Pp. 106-7)

He goes on to warn that "Hell has made three principal attacks on the Way of Romantic Love. The dangerous assumptions produced are: (1) the assumption that it will naturally be everlasting; (2) the assumption that it is personal; (3) the assumption that it is sufficient" (pp. 108-9). And so he moves to his conclusion:

But, independent of any personal error, the vision has remained. It is not limited to love between the sexes, nor to any love. The use of the word (so spoilt has it become) in some sense colours it with the horrid tint of a false adoration and a pseudo-piety. But grace remains grace whatever fruits are grown from it. The experience of communicated humility and goodwill is the experience of the grace of reality and of the kingdom. The kingdom came down from heaven and was incarnate; since then and perhaps (because of it) before then, it is beheld through and in a carnality of joy. The beloved—person or thing—becomes the Mother of Love; Love is born in the soul; it may have its passion there; it may have its resurrection. It has its own divine nature united with our undivine nature. In such a doctrine the Gospels take on other meanings. The light that lighteth every man is seen without as well as within. But that, by definition, is the nature of the kingdom. (Pp. 112-13)

10. "Behold, I make all things new" (Revelation 21:5).

SEQUEL

Where, then, in all of this, did his view of marriage stand, now that his relationship with Phyllis was petering out? He was still living at home with Florence, and though life there had been very difficult indeed for both, she had with great good sense kept his home going for him to return to. The Beatrician vision that came to him from Dante can hardly have failed to bring back to him his own first meeting with Florence in 1908, and the writing of *The Silver Stair*.[11] My guess is that the re-creation of his marriage began during this time, as may be exhibited by Williams's dedication of *He Came Down from Heaven*: "To Michal[12] by whom I began to study the doctrine of glory."

From this time also, I think, dates a realization that his experience of Phyllis, though not to be denied, had been a dead-end. In mid-1939 he wrote in a letter to me: "I add a personal note—I suspect I am freer. It occurred to me one night that one really ought *not* to go about feeling that one debäcle—even a serious debäcle—was quite enough and that one's life had—what shall I say? done its share! God send no more! still, you see what I mean?"

In *He Came Down from Heaven* he writes that it is false to assume that the Beatrician state is everlasting.

"The right faith is that we believe and confess" that it is eternal but is not everlastingly visible. . . . [I]t may be expected to return quickly as was Christ by the Church. It may not. Its authority remains unimpaired. The emotional vows, however, springing from its original state, do not at all times appear so possible or desirable. On the other hand, it seems to be true that there is at first a very strong desire in the two lovers to maintain and conduct for ever this experiment towards *caritas* between themselves, and certainly some kind of pledged fidelity would seem to be a condition of the experiment. The Church has maintained that (under certain conditions) exchanged vows of this kind should be regarded as final. It has even maintained (justly) that, as in certain cases, the state of love leads to marriage, so marriage can lead to a more advanced state of love, and since, on the whole hypothesis, this is the only desirable thing, it may be right in its discipline. (The natural tendency to falsify evidence in favour of a point of view does not perhaps

11. The coincidence between "Florence" and Beatrice "the Florentine girl" may have helped.
12. Williams's domestic name for his wife.

83

prevail more strongly here than elsewhere.) But the matter of marriage is a subject different from the present and of too lofty a nature to be contented with a paragraph. The appearance of the glory is temporary; the authority of the glory towards pure love is everlasting; the quality of the glory is eternal, such as the heavens have in Christ. (Pp. 109-10)

Until his re-discovery of Dante, he seems to have regarded the formulation of romantic theology as his own discovery. In the letter to Phyllis I quoted earlier, for instance, he says that although the "thesis was metaphysically formulated before the Celian Star rose," it was she who enabled him fully to understand it. But from *He Came Down from Heaven* to the end of his life, his own discoveries are subsumed into Dante's, and it is Dante's that thenceforth he expounds.

His next book, *The Descent of the Dove*, published by Longmans Green in 1939, was also theological. In it we find described, somewhat acidly, the Church's views on marriage: "[The Church] lost any really active tradition of marriage itself as a way of the soul. This we have still to recover; it is, no doubt, practised in a million homes, but it can hardly be said to have been diagrammatized or taught by the authorities. Monogamy and meekness have been taught instead" (p. 14).

In early Christian days there were the hermits. The old heretical Gnostic view that matter was evil had no doubt affected them, and its related belief, Manichaeanism, also did so. "It is due to Manichaeanism," he says, "that there has grown up in Christendom . . . the vague suggestion that the body has somehow fallen farther than the soul. It was certainly nourished within the Church by the desert ascetics—especially in their ingenuous repudiation of sex. . . . Sex—the poor ignorant creatures thought—was one of the greatest, most subtle, and most lasting of all distractions; nor had the Church . . . shown any striking sign of intending to exhibit it as sometimes the greatest, most splendid, and most authoritative of all inducements" (p. 56).

Nevertheless, "counterchecking the asceticism it admired, the formal doctrine of Christendom concerning matter remained constant," and the two methods, the Affirmative Way and the Negative Way, coexisted. "The Way of Affirmation was to develop great art and romantic love and marriage and philosophy and social justice; the Way of Rejection was to break out continually in the profound mystical documents of the soul" (pp. 57-58). Later the working out of Canon

Law began to regulate the relations between man and woman from the moment they met: "The first inviting smile . . . brought the two parties under its operative shadow" (p. 124). And whereas before the Council of Trent the presence of a priest was not required for the validity of the sacrament of marriage, Canon Law changed that.

All the same, the medieval Church felt nervous, not so much about sex or marriage as about passion, whether romantic or otherwise, for it involved, it thought, a dangerous suspension of intellectual activity. "From this point of view," Williams points out, "passion towards a man's wife was as bad as passion towards somebody else's wife. . . . Marriage therefore might easily become an occasion of sin, only redeemable by a strong devotion towards 'justice' . . . ; the partners had to be 'fair' towards each other; they had to exchange permitted, but only natural, satisfactions" (p. 130), and passion was out of bounds.

Then arose another idea, especially among poets, that passion "precisely excited and illuminated the intellect" and that "such a passion could exist as or in marriage. The idea of marriage as a way of the soul became a possibility. Passion was no longer to be only a morally dubious because unintellectual quality of marriage, which was itself but a degree of justice working itself out in the world. The discovery of a supernatural justice between two lovers was passion's justification, and yet not only justification, but its very cause. There was vision (or conversion) and there was co-inherence and there was faith and hope and the Christian diagram of universal good-will. . . . In certain states of romantic love the Holy Spirit has deigned to reveal, as it were, the Christ-hood of two individuals each to other" (p. 131).

At this point Williams comes again to Dante, devoting eight pages to summarizing Dante's thought on romantic theology, this time discarding the *Convivio* to give space to the *Comedy*. "The *New Life*," he says, "exhibits the passion of Dante for Beatrice. But the *Comedy* exhibits the passion of Beatrice for Dante" (p. 133).

War came in September 1939. Charles Williams was evacuated to Oxford with his office and lodged with a Press friend, Gerard Hopkins. Florence decided to remain in their London flat. Hopkins had once been Phyllis's lover, and some years back Williams had undergone a storm of jealousy on his account. That they could now share lodgings surely indicates that Williams's passion for her had ended, though its validity remained. Again Florence's decision, however arrived at, was wise. Williams, already on his way back to her as a result of his Dantean experience, was able to live his own intellectual life at Oxford, a fructiferous life which included his friendships with C. S. Lewis, J. R. R. Tolkien, and the other Inklings, and a wide range of lecturing and article-writing. Yet he could, and did, return home at weekends, and indeed felt it to be home. In addition, he wrote over 600 letters to Florence between late 1939 and his death in May 1945. I myself know from long ago how valuable such regular letter-writing is to lovers in deepening, widening, and renewing their love. So it was, I think, with Williams; in August 1941 he wrote to Florence: "I love you more now, both because I like to and because I ought to, and because I *do*. The third is the best cause—fortunate that it holds."

In the same year, Williams wrote *Religion and Love in Dante*, reprinted in full in this volume. It was first published in 1941, during what was perhaps the worst period for Britain of the second World War, by the Dacre Press of Westminster, London, as No. 6 of the Dacre Papers.

Set out in it is romantic theology to the point he had taken it since writing *Outlines of Romantic Theology* seventeen years earlier. Since this previously scarce little booklet is now made available to all, I shall comment on it only briefly. Love-in-marriage has now been firmly given the pre-eminence: "It is true the Dantean way is not confined to marriage, otherwise its principles could not apply to any known love— in marriage, in the family, in friendship, which they probably do. But it is also true that marriage is a unique opportunity of following that way. Marriage becomes a Way of the Soul. It is the elucidation of that kind of Way of the Soul with which Dante was concerned" (p. 92 herein).

We get such phrases as: "no second experience can, of itself, destroy the value of a first experience. . . . Dante has to become the thing he has seen. He has to become, by his own will, the *caritas* which was, by God's will, awakened in him at the smile of Beatrice; he has to be faithful to that great communication in the days when Beatrice does not smile" (pp. 96-97).

We also now get a statement that, even if the Way of Romantic Love is not one to be followed side by side with others, it can—indeed should—include others. Williams refers to "Dante's concern with general life, with, as one may say, the City of Man. . . . The principles of this . . . are a necessary part of the Beatrician Way. Politics are, or should be, a part of *caritas*; they are the matter to which the form of *caritas* must be applied" (p. 97).

Most important of all, we learn that if we hold fast to the Beatrician vision through emotional and physical loss, we can be saved by it. But we have to learn how it works—and so we are led through hell, to see how it does not work, and purgatory, to see how it can work, to paradise where it does work.

He ends the little book in clear affirmation: anyone who falls in love, and experiences in doing so a trace of what Dante—or Williams—experienced, should not neglect it, for "if we neglect it, we shall neglect, both for ourselves and for others, a Way of Sanctity. Marriage might be the most common exposition of the Way; as, no doubt, in many unknown homes it is" (p. 111). The Way includes all potentialities, very much including sex: "The division is not between the Eros of the flesh and the Agape of the soul; it is between the moment of love which sinks into hell and the moment which rises to the in-Godding. . . . This is the unique and lasting mystery of the Way" (p. 111).

Two years after *Religion and Love in Dante*, Williams published what I think is his best book, *The Figure of Beatrice*, in which he examines fully the Beatrician vision.[13] He does so in terms of Dante as the greatest in literature, but he also pays tribute to that early influence upon himself, Coventry Patmore, and to the poet who, in the end, meant more to him than Shakespeare, Milton, or any poet other than Dante—Wordsworth. The book should be read, indeed, possessed to re-read, by everyone who seeks to follow the Way of Romantic Love. To summarize it would be impossible. A year later, in 1944, appeared his second book of Arthurian poems, *The Region of the Summer Stars*, which I think was written with clearer vision than the first.

These were, I think, personal fulfillments. Charles Williams had written *Outlines of Romantic Theology* in 1924 as a statement of what romantic love, before and in marriage, had taught him, just before he fell in love again. He had worked through that second experience, without denying either it or his continuing marriage, and come out on

---

13. The book was published by Faber & Faber, who as Faber & Gwyer had so nearly published *Outlines of Romantic Theology*.

the other side. He had realized that both experiences were valid, and therefore that romantic love could be worked out within or without marriage. He had practiced it with Florence, then with Phyllis, and in his last years he came back to a renewal of *l'antica fiamma*, the original flame.

Thus in his end was his beginning. In Chapter VI of *Outlines of Romantic Theology* he had glimpsed intimations of what was to be learned from the *Morte d'Arthur* and from Dante about romantic theology. Some twenty years later, in his greatest book, *The Figure of Beatrice*, and in the second volume of his Taliessin poems, he explored the same subject more deeply. His marriage to Florence bridged the many years between. In spite of all that had happened in those years, in the end I think Williams could say:

> Thy firmness makes my circle just,
> And makes me end where I begun.[14]

14. John Donne, A *Valediction: Forbidding Mourning*, lines 35-36.

RELIGION AND LOVE IN DANTE

The Theology of Romantic Love

Religion and Love in Dante:
The Theology of Romantic Love

The title of this paper is not intended to propagate Christianity by arousing a factitious sense of the excitements of Theology. The assurance that Christianity is or ought to be thrilling, whether as an adventure or a catastrophe, is in danger perhaps of being a little overdone. Christianity, like all religions, is, frequently, almost unmitigated boredom or even a slow misery, in which the command to rejoice always is the most difficult of all.

The word 'romantic' is used here in some such defining sense as the words Pastoral, Moral, Dogmatic, or Mystical; it means theology as applied to a particular state—that of romantic love. I am not pretending that this is a theological treatise; it is no more than an opening of the possibility. It is convenient to begin that opening by considering the work of a great poet because the accuracy of poets presents us with definite statements; and convenient to begin with Dante because Dante is generally accepted as a great Christian poet, and there will be few doubts as to his orthodoxy. Also because he did the thing better than anyone else. The Dacre Press has already published one paper on Dante, treating his thought in special relation to the present time.* The present paper proposes only to discuss it in relation to that human experience of 'falling-in-love', from which Dante's own imagination began to work and the process and final possibilities of which he explored.

* *Dante and the Present War.*

91

Two points must first be raised. The first is that this, it will be said, has often been done before. That, to an extent, is true. But it may be answered (i) that it can hardly be done too often, (ii) that we do not hitherto seem to have learnt much by what has been done. We seem to be able to denounce divorce much more easily than we can explain marriage. It is true the Dantean way is not confined to marriage, otherwise its principles could not apply to any known love—in marriage, in the family, in friendship, which they probably do. But it is also true that marriage is a unique opportunity of following that way. Marriage becomes a Way of the Soul. It is the elucidation of that kind of Way of the Soul with which Dante was concerned.

The second point is the use of the word 'Imagination'. It is generally employed to mean a vague and uncontrolled fancy. In fact, it needs only right direction, and it may then become power. Wordsworth said it was 'absolute power'. It may become the union of the mind and the heart with a particular vision. Certain of the poets, by their own particular visions, have supplied us with a pattern of life. This, certainly, is only part of their special energy, and whether their pattern is useful to us or not has nothing to do with our judgement or enjoyment of them as poets. But to understand their patterns has. It is afterwards for us to decide whether one or other pattern is a pattern on which we choose to meditate. We shall, therefore, be concerned here not so much with the consideration of Dante as a poet, as with that pattern of life which is a part of his poetry, and which he made evident to us by means of his poetry. It need not, of course, be applicable to our own lives in every detail, but the general principle may be. It is realistic or it is nothing; it is accurate or it is nothing. If it is regarded merely as a beautiful poetic dream, the dynamics of it will be lost. 'The poet and the dreamer are distinct.'

Dante's work, for our present purpose, is divisible into three groups, (i) the *New Life*, (ii) the *Banquet*, the *On Monarchy*, and other prose works, (iii) the *Comedy*, which is in three parts, *(a) Hell, (b) Purgatory, (c) Paradise*. I use the English names for convenience. The *Comedy* is usually called the *Divine Comedy*, but Dante himself gave it the shorter name; the adjective was added later. The beginning of the whole vision is at the beginning of the first book, the *New Life*. It is concerned with what, in our modern language, is called 'Boy meeting

Girl'. At the age of nine Dante met at a party another child, almost nine, by whose appearance he was thrilled; he met her again and again, and at the age of eighteen he realized that he was deeply in love. That is the simple statement; a young man met a young woman, somewhere about the year 1283, in the streets of Florence, and he fell in love. She, so far as we know, did not. That, however, was an accident of their personal lives. What follows, speaking generally, is to the very end of his work an account of what Dante thought, said, and did about this remarkable state of affairs. Had Beatrice, which was either her name or the name he gave her, fallen in love with him, the Way that he followed might have been less or more difficult; it would perhaps have been different in certain respects, but it could hardly have been very different in its essential nature.

He was then, in the most literal sense, 'shocked' by this experience, and (as poets will) he made immediate attempts to understand and define it to himself. It may be said here at once that the whole possibility of Dante's vision being useful to us depends on what view we take of 'falling in love'. Dante, except that he was a great poet, was apparently a normal young man—selfish, proud, hot-tempered, sexually alert, busy with a lot of affairs, especially with politics. He was born in 1265; he did his military service at 24; he was, as one might say, Mayor of the City at 35; he was an omnivorous reader, interested in art and science and theology. There was, except for that capacity of ordering his vision in great poetry, nothing unusual about him. But it is, of course, open to us to deny that most young people fall in love as Dante did, and that they see a particular person of the opposite sex in a blaze of beauty and goodness. It may be that all that is only a literary tradition. I do not myself think it is; I think it is a normal human emotion. It may or may not be accompanied, or very quickly followed, by the direct sexual emotion; generally it is. In Dante's case it certainly was; we know this because he says so. He discovered that the sight of Beatrice produced three re-actions in him. He attributed them (as was the habit of the physiological science of his day, and therefore also a literary habit) to three centres of the human body—the heart, the brain, and the liver. The heart, where (to him) 'the spirit of life' dwelled, exclaimed to him, at that first meeting: 'Behold a god stronger than I, who is to come and rule over me'. The brain declared: 'Now your beatitude has appeared to

93

you'. And the liver (where natural emotions, such as sex, inhabited) said: 'O misery! how I shall be disturbed henceforward!'

He is, it seems, 'satisfied' by Beatrice; his sensations, his emotions, his ideas, his faith, coalesce. Perfection in some strange sense exists, and walks down the street of Florence to meet him. She is 'the youngest of the Angels'; her image in his thought 'is an exultation of Love to subdue him', yet so perfect that Love never acts without 'the faithful counsel of reason, wherever such counsel was useful to be heard'; she is 'the destroyer of all evil and the queen of all good'; she is the equivalent of heaven itself. I will repeat again that it is for Dante's readers to determine whether they think this to be a normal state for a young man in love or not. I do not say universal; I will not claim that it is true of everyone. But if it is true of a very large number, as it seems on the evidence to be, then we had better determine what kind of attention we are going to give it. If it is this which often leads to marriage, then we shall not understand marriage unless we understand this; if it is this which sometimes breaks up marriage, then still more we ought to understand it. If, as in Dante's own personal case, it neither leads to marriage nor breaks up marriage, then it may still be one of the more important human experiences, as it was to Dante.

The *New Life* continues to give an account of this relationship. It was, objectively, a very slender relationship. Beatrice and Dante were certainly on speaking terms, but that is about all we know. We know that because at one time she had heard tales about him and she cut him dead in the street.* It is this incident which provides him with an opportunity to describe what meeting her meant to him—what meeting the boy or girl has (it is our present thesis) meant to thousands of similar girls or boys. He says that when she met him in the street and said good-morning, he was so highly moved that he was, for the moment, in a state of complete good-will, complete *caritas* towards everyone. If anyone had at that moment done him an injury, he would necessarily have forgiven him. He has not only fallen in love; he is, strictly, 'in love'. He is aware of that beyond everything; 'if anyone had asked me a

---

* I am aware of the literary convention of Dante's time, a convention adequately and effectively discussed in Mr. C. S. Lewis's *Allegory of Love*. But a literary convention is, at its best, a means of passion.

question I should have been able to answer only "Love".' This would sound sentimental were it not for Dante's careful use of other words. It is a 'Love' which necessarily forgives injuries; or rather, it does so because it is indeed Love. And therefore he calls her salutation 'blessed', because it is beatitude which it inspires. In fact, he becomes for one moment in his soul that Perfection which he has observed in Beatrice.

I repeat that Dante was no sentimentalist. He knew that in that fortunate state he experienced, according to its degree, beatitude. But he does not suggest that that state is fixed in him. He adored the Glory in Beatrice, as thousands of us have; he became the Glory in himself by a simple communication of grace. Love, charity, *agape*, was for the moment inevitable. But it was to be a long time before he could himself become that state permanently. It was indeed, as we can see from a consideration of all his work, his whole problem: could he indeed become the Glory which he saw and by which for a moment he had been transfused? It was his problem as it has been and remains the life-problem of many others. The rest of Dante's work is a pattern of the Way. 'I have been', he said soon after that description, 'at that point of life beyond which he who passes cannot return'; and this indeed is the description of such a 'falling in love'—it is a region from which no creature returns afterwards. One is never the same again.

The *New Life* has in it many very pleasant and agreeable lesser incidents not unlike those of any young man in love. He wrote verse about her (but it happened to be good verse); he tried to avoid being publicly supposed to be attracted by her. But the next passage to which there is room here to draw attention is a kind of curious meditation— possibly of very high significance, possibly not; the reader must judge. He sees one day a girl coming towards him (all Dante's devotion to Beatrice did not prevent him noticing such other incidents) whose name was Joan. She was also called by her friends Primavera, or Spring. Behind her, at a little distance, was Beatrice; and Dante was struck by the thought that Joan was going before Beatrice as John the Precursor went before our Lord. Unless this is serious, it is almost profane. If it is serious, it is the beginning of a very high mystical identity. Beatrice is not our Lord. But Beatrice has been throughout precisely the vehicle of Love, of sexual love and of the vision in sexual love. She has awakened in Dante a celestial reverie; she has appeared to him the very carriage of beauty and goodness; she has, unknowingly, communicated to him an experience of *caritas*. These are the properties of Almighty Love. What Dante is now doing is to identify the power which reposed in Beatrice with the nature of our Lord. Love had been (as he himself said) a quality; now, hardly defining it, he is on the point of seeing it as precisely the Person of Love. In that moment he justified all future lovers in a similar moment.

It is impossible, or at least undesirable, to follow this spiritual identification further here; such a study would have to be separate. We must return to the more exact intellectual meaning of the incidents, and pass on at once to the Death of Beatrice. Dante heard of it when, having left Florence on business, he was engaged in composing a poem, and he breaks off with a phrase from the Lamentations of Jeremiah: 'How doth the city sit solitary that was full of people! how is she become as a widow that was great among the nations!'

There is no reason to suppose that the Death of Beatrice was, in Dante's own life, anything else than the death of Beatrice. She died young—she, the single girl who was the high and unmeriting cause of so much, whose single face justified, by the art of her lover, so many other faces. The women who have seriously affected great art have been few, and fewer those who have affected great theology in great art— happy if (as probably Beatrice did not) they knew of what they were the cause, happier if they took an active part in the result. She died, and even her death became vastly significant. For that sudden young death stands to us not only as an actual death of an actual girl, the princely gaiety that smiled at Dante in Florence, but also as a vanishing of Perfection. It has been, through all time, part of the monotonous admonition of the old to the young that such rapt visions do not last, and far too often the discouraged old have implied that the mere fact of the quick passage of the vision means that it was in some sense unreliable, untrustworthy, valueless. It is false; no second experience can, of itself, destroy the value of a first experience. Yet aged imbecility has this much to be said for it—the particular Glory of the first 'falling-in-love', the living sense of Perfection, does seem to be withdrawn. Time and habit veil it perhaps. But I would rather choose to believe that it is not merely so, but that the Glory which attended the vehicle of Love operates at the will of Love. Dante has to become the

96

thing he has seen. He has to become, by his own will, the *caritas* which was, by God's will, awakened in him at the smile of Beatrice; he has to be faithful to that great communication in the days when Beatrice does not smile. Or, if she had lived and smiled, then when she had seemed to exhibit only natural joy and not supernatural power. 'There hath passed away', wrote Wordsworth of another revelation, 'a Glory from the earth'. Religion itself knows such withdrawals; 'the dark night' is asserted to be an inevitable stage of the Way. Dante knew the death of Beatrice, and many other young lovers have known the disappearance of the peculiar Beatrician quality. This is the meaning of the death in the whole pattern. It is not, however, an unfortunate accident which is a conclusion. It is a state of being, a quenching of sensitive knowledge, which is a necessary—or all but necessary—part of the Way of Romantic Love.

Beatrice, then, dies; and for the present purpose the book of the *New Life* must be left at that point.* The second group of Dante's writings need not detain us long. The *Banquet* is a philosophical discussion; the *On Monarchy* a political, and the *On the Common Speech* a literary. They represent Dante's concern with general life, with, as one may say, the City of Man, especially *On Monarchy*. The principles of this have been already discussed in the other Dacre Paper (*Dante and the Present War*), and all that need be said here is that they are a necessary part of the Beatrician way. Politics are, or should be, a part of *caritas*; they are the matter to which the form of *caritas* must be applied. The *On Monarchy* is Dante exercising his capacities, the capacities illuminated by the *New Life*, but not so much concerned with Beatrice directly as with the whole effort of human relationships. They too failed in fact, as far as Dante's own life was concerned; he was exiled, condemned to death, and disreputed in Florence. This was perhaps an even greater contradiction of his vision

---

* I deliberately do not here discuss the problems of the other lady—the Lady at the Window, as she is called, because in so short a space I wish to keep to the main path of the Way. If she were actual (as I suppose), she was in some sense a re-expression of the Glory. But then certainly it cannot have been she on whose account Beatrice rebukes Dante in the *Purgatory*. The attributions to her in the *Banquet* are more intellectual than those in the *New Life*, and she is more closely identified with Philosophy. But that is what we should expect from Dante's developing mind; she is more closely identified with Philosophy because she is, in fact, more apt to be analyzed philosophically.

than the death of Beatrice; with Beatrice the visible Good had disappeared, but in Florence the possible Good had been betrayed.

These two facts, which were true of his external life, seem to have been true also of his interior. Beatrice had been taken away from his sight and he had also in some sense lost fidelity to her. The exact nature of this loss of fidelity can be conveniently discussed later. It was at this time, in exile and conscious of his own sin, but conscious no less of his own poetic genius and of what he believed to be his duty, that he set to work on the *Comedy*.

The opening of the first part of the *Comedy*, of the *Hell*, is a great and complex account of this situation. Dante 'refinds' himself; he becomes again conscious of himself. It is the morning of Good Friday, of the Betrayal and the Passion. He is middle-aged; he is lost in a dark wood; he is on a path 'more bitter than death'. Everything has gone wrong, and he has gone wrong. He sees before him a great mountain which he obscurely identifies with a desired happiness—'the occasion and beginning of our Joy'. It is not, then, further defined; a kind of nightmare is on him, and one does not define further the vivid apparitions of nightmare. He tries to reach it; all will then be well; but he cannot; three wild beasts appear on the slopes and drive him back again into the wild wood. These beasts, as in nightmare (and also in poetry), are several things at the same time. They are beasts; they are also certain evils—Lechery, Pride, Avarice; they are also the three chief periods of human life displayed by those evils. The Panther is gay and beautiful and speedy; the Lion is strong and fierce; the She-Wolf, terrible beyond the others, is fierce with an insatiable hunger. Youth and Middle Age and Old Age—and of all these Old Age, lean and insatiably greedy, is the worst. It is she who prevents the ascent and destroys what has been. Beyond is the unattainable skiey mountain, something more than temporal; behind is the dark wood of his lost misery, and to that darkness he is inevitably returning.

What interferes? The love of Beatrice. The *New Life* had been about the love of Dante for Beatrice, but the *Comedy* is about the love of Beatrice for Dante. She is made aware of his peril by the intervention, through St. Lucy, of the Mother of God; and she immediately acts. All that follows depends on her. This is worth noting because it is a preparation for what does follow much later in the poem. Beatrice's love of her lover may be of a more advanced kind than his for her, but it is no less passionate. When she rebukes him it is he whom she rebukes; when, in the *Paradise*, she delivers what seem rather like lectures on the movement of the stars and all that sort of thing, it is only because he very much wants to know and she happens to know; it is for his pleasure rather than hers. She teases him, she scolds him, she calls him by names of love; and in the very end it is he only at whom her eyes gaze before they plunge into the mystery of God himself. She is a divine thing, but she is also, still and always, the Florentine girl.

She moves then to her lover's rescue. But he does not at the moment know that. Great and marvellous though his experience of her had been in that 'falling-in-love', it had not been his only experience, and Dante was far too intelligent to pretend that it had. What appears to him in that nightmare, and seems for the first moment to add to the nightmare, is a kind of ghostly figure who may be anything, and whose voice, when it first speaks aloud in that disastrous forest, is hoarse from long disuse. Spectral and awful it looms, but it is Dante's only hope, in that hideous simultaneous appearance which life has put on: he appeals to it. It answers; it promises help, and presently—O dispersal of the horrid dream!—it names Mantua, Virgil's city. It *is* Virgil: 'My Master and my Author'—'Maestro e autore'. Now Virgil, besides being Virgil, is also everything good that is not Beatrice. 'Autore' is 'author' in Milton's sense; 'my author and disposer'. He is, particularly, poetry, the source of Dante's own style. It is clear therefore that it is very fitting that he should be sent by Beatrice—or rather not sent, for no command has been laid upon him; it is his own courtesy which has moved him. But also, since poetry is not religion, it is very fitting that he should not lead Dante into Paradise. Virgil—poetry—may exhibit visions, and initiate conduct; it cannot be religion. This is not, of course, to say that we should, when we are writing poetry, put religion before poetry; poetry is absolute in its own place, and even Beatrice cannot command it. The voice of Virgil is his own.

The message which he brings is that the only way of safety from the she-wolf of Avarice and Age is to see 'the eternal'—the principles of the universe. These are to be shown in the three places of the dead, (i) those who desire the second death, (ii) those who are contented in the fire, (iii) the blessed. Dante accepts the vision and the way (which

Beatrice has brought to him): 'Poet, by the God that poetry in itself cannot reach, lead on.'

The 'blind' world of Hell into which Dante and Virgil now enter is an ordered descent through a number of circles of sinners. This descent can be understood, as all great poetry can be, in many different ways. But one of those ways is that of the particular Beatrician vision; that is, the experience of 'falling in love' is here followed to its distant and dreadful end in a complete betrayal of itself. The first circle belongs to the great pagans who could not, as Dante saw it, be saved; it belongs, certainly, precisely to poetry and philosophy which cannot, of them-selves, lead to salvation. It is where Virgil himself dwells. But after that, in the second circle of hell (but the first punishment of sin) we come to the sufferings of the incontinent, or those who have loved by their own indulgence against the moral law. With two of these Dante speaks; they are the unhappy lovers Paolo and Francesca. Now it is true that these two have sinned in their love, but it is also true that their sin is possible to all lovers, moral or immoral. It is a too great indulgence, a too long lingering in permitted delight, a lawless concentration on each other. Dante is so overcome with pity at the sight of them that he faints; and that faint is led up to by every circumstance of tenderness. What is sinful in Paolo and Francesca is, as one might say, only just sinful. Their love is beautiful, moving, faithful: what is wrong with it? Only the prolonga-tion of the self-indulged moment. Love is lazy. But that laziness, though it is the most touching thing in hell, is yet the very opening to all hell. For what, in the very order of hell, follows?

The love of Paolo and Francesca had been lovely and mutual; the next circle carries indulgence a step further. It is the circle of the gluttons, and it is clear that here gluttony has, as Dante distinctly stated that all his work had, a symbolical interpretation. Gluttony is, no doubt, gluttony, but also it is gluttony in everything, and that no longer with a companion, in a kind of sharing of even sin, but separately, but alone. The next step to preferring oneself in 'the two of us' against all else is to prefer oneself alone. And this leads, inevitably, on that lost and secret path, to hatred of others who have their own other desires; and first of all, in the vision, we are shown the soul contending against other souls, the lover of himself against the lovers of their own selves, or even the soul against itself. It is as they pass from the circle of misers and spendthrifts—the disordered desire to preserve fighting against the disordered desire to enjoy—that Virgil exclaims: 'Now let us descend into even greater misery', and they go on to the circle of mere anger. Joy has disappeared and intellect is disappearing; they enter the marsh of *accidie*, of gloom, where those who hated 'the sweet air and the sun' lie gurgling in the bubbling mud.

All these are, no doubt, separate sins, but they are also in some sense a development of the same sin, the sin of indulging oneself in love instead of devoting oneself to the duty of love, the perverse and selfish twisting of the 'falling-in-love' to nothing but one's own satisfaction. For every mistake made on the Way of Romantic Love there is pardon and grace; for the deliberate and continued perversion of it, there can be, by the nature of things, no pardon—'neither here nor in the world to come'.

The 'greater misery' deepens. Something more like definite hate appears; the travellers are attacked; as they reach the wall of the infernal City of Dis the gates are shut against them and the devils threaten them. Something looks over the wall of the City against the sight of which Virgil covers Dante's eyes. The dark air is lit by the ever-burning mosques of hell; above them the storm whirls round the immense but narrowing funnel of the abyss; before them are the walls of iron; and below is the unknown hell of even worse horrors. When at last the poets enter the City, they are in the place of heretics. What is heresy? the clinging to a particular thought or idea because it is one's own, although it is against the known decision of the Church—the disintegrity of the intellect, the justification to oneself of error and evil. Here that self-indulgence has gone very far—'and much more than you can see', says Virgil, 'the burning tombs of the heretics lie laden.' Beyond are the other circles of the deliberate sinners against love by force or fraud. Eros has turned wholly against itself; it is now fully that old she-wolf 'lean with insatiable cravings'. 'The pollution of all the world' rises to meet them; the great torments open on every side. There is no space here to detail them. Only it may be remembered that though they are all separate, yet they are all one. It is one soul, as well as many, which is chaotic with its horrid longings; the soul which, among many interpretations, can be seen to be that which had once loved only a little in the wrong way and been content; it is more—it is the soul, or might be, as Dante very well knew, which had once seen the beauty and experienced the grace communicated by the girl's face in the streets of Florence, or any other city. There is one incident which reveals it. In one of the loathsome ditches lie a people covered by human excrement, and among them a certain woman—'a foul and dishevelled drab, scratching herself with filthy nails, and restless—now squatting, now standing'. It is Thais, the harlot. There had been harlots far above, in the circle of the incontinent—Cleopatra, and Helen, and others; why is Thais here? because she is lost in the filth of flattery for her own gain. The frank harlots are the least of all sinners; she among the greater. One of her lovers (this is the story Dante quotes) had said to her: 'Are you very grateful to me?' and she answered: 'Beyond all measure.' She had, that is, pretended in her harlotry to what is exactly true in the holy innocence of the Beatrician vision. Dante and Thais both said in effect: 'I am infinitely grateful'. But Dante meant 'infinitely' and Thais did not. She scratches herself therefore for ever in the excrement of which her words were the exact image.

At the very bottom of hell everything changes. Noise ceases; fire vanishes; diseases disappear. Almost a different kind of life appears— the life of the utterly damned. Damnation itself lives, in so far as it can live; the perverse contradiction of all good. Here the damned are almost one with Hell. At the beginning the vision of the beloved had awoke Dante to courtesy and humility and goodwill; and from Beatrice he had moved to an apprehension of the mass of men, and the Divine City. Virgil and Beatrice had stood for everything, and the plain of ice on which the poets now find themselves is the opposite of both Virgil and Beatrice. Tears themselves are frozen within the eyes; 'their weeping does not allow them to weep'. There the souls lie wholly covered by ice, and are indistinguishable; no-one speaks; instead of speech there is the wind of the air disturbed only by the monotonous beating of Satan's wings. These are the final traitors to their 'lords and benefactors'. This is the end of the way which had begun, so almost excusably, with Paolo and Francesca, the spiritual treachery to which that little indulgence must, unrepented, eventually lead; here is Satan, 'the creature who was once so beautiful,' and is now 'the guilty worm which pierces the world'. This, certainly, is what love, even the love of Beatrice, or of any woman or any man, may become. 'It is time for parting; all is seen.'

The poets pass from this cannibalism of the spirit to the second great vision—the Purgatory-Paradise. Dante is to be shown the quality of eternity. Hell is eternity without the quality of eternity; that is, it is mere monotonous and everlasting repetition. The new discovery is to be of repentance and re-formation, but it is the love-planet Venus which still presides. It begins (like Hell) with a single moment of love. Dante meets his friend Casella, who sings to him one of Dante's own poems, a poem which opened the third book of the *Banquet*. The first line is: 'Love that discourses to me in my mind', and Dante insists on the 'in my mind' for it is there that this affection for truth and virtue exists. The aspect of the beloved 'aids our faith', just as it 'renovates nature'. But the mind has to work on it, and so has faith, and it is this which, it seems, Paolo and Francesca have not done. There is a little delay even here. Dante and all the souls, and even Virgil, are so held by the singing that they stand listening, until the Guardian of the Place interferes— 'How now, slow spirits! what delay is this? On to the Mount, strip yourselves of the slough, and let God be manifest to you', and all skirr off like frightened doves.

It is Pride that is the sin purged in the first terrace of Purgatory, where moving towers of stone seem to appear, until it is found that they are sinners carrying great weights on their backs. The first intention of anyone who knows that love which Beatrice has awakened must be to rid himself of himself. The soul illuminated by that young love-vision has to make haste; it cannot itself become those virtues which were for an instant communicated to it until it attends to other than itself. But when this is done, it finds that the next purging is of Envy; without freedom from that there can be no development of love, and just as in hell the gluttony of love leads to hatred of others, so here the envious souls have their eyes sewn up, so that they cannot see others and are blind to the facts of things. 'O mortal race, why do you set your hearts to exclude partnership?' This is the second demand of Purgatory that love, being humble, should be open to include; that is, that the emotion aroused by the salutation of Beatrice should become a principle of life. This is the definition of the true romantic way. It is perhaps significant that it is while Virgil is explaining that 'the more souls that love so much the more love' that he promises that the sight of Beatrice in heaven will explain all. So, they are on the third terrace where a harsh smoke hides those who were guilty of Anger, and at the beginning and end of this terrace is a kind of ecstasy of gentleness, a proper introduction to what happens on the fourth, Virgil's great discourse on the nature of love. Half the vision is seen; half the poem is done. It turns, as it were, on itself to move faster to its end.

Love, says Virgil in his analysis, can never turn against itself; man cannot hate himself or his Maker; whom then? his neighbour—by deliberate evil heart or by failure of love. True love may be sluggish, or it may be confused in its object, and lack proportion. 'Set love in order.' 'All loves that move you arise from necessity, but power to control is in you. This noble virtue Beatrice means by free-will; have this in mind if she speaks of it.' Free-will is the right control of confused love. While they are speaking the terrace is full of the purgation of sloth; many souls running with great speed. It is, in a sense, the first prospect of Paradise, and there remain but the terraces of Avarice and Gluttony and Lechery to pass, these three mounting towards heaven in that order as in hell they descend in the reverse order. It is while on this journey that Dante takes an opportunity to state the realism of his own love-poetry. 'I am one', he says, 'who when love breathes in me observe it, and in the manner it dictates within go on to expound it.' It was the claim of Dante to be accurate, as it was his delight. He certainly never supposed himself to be dreaming of a false spirituality, he whose initiation was accomplished by mortal eyes.

The last terrace is a terrace of flame in which the lustful are purged, and it is when the poets have reached the end of this terrace and have to pass through a wall of fire that Virgil encourages Dante by the mention of those eyes. 'My sweet Father, to comfort me, spoke of Beatrice as he went forward, saying: "Already I seem to see her eyes".' It is the last purification from an actual sin; the whole will has been healed and restored. Virgil's great line consummates the whole: 'I crown and mitre thee over thyself'. The forest of the Earthly Paradise stretches before him: he has, here, indeed re-found himself. It is in this renewal of himself and of earth that the Florentine girl again appears.

It is now in the Earthly Paradise, after the sins have been obliterated and the virtues re-established, that the full supernatural validity of Beatrice begins to be expressed. It had, one might suppose, been made sufficiently clear in the *New Life*, and certainly if that were all that remained to us of Dante's work it would be sufficient for the religious encouragement of all lovers. But we now know that, in addition to that young enthusiasm the mature mind of Dante did not wish to establish any contrary doctrine. He takes particular care to identify the processional figure who now appears, drawn by the celestial Two-Natured Gryphon (half Lion and half Eagle) who is Christ, and accompanied by Angels, Virtues, Prophets, and Evangelists, with the very Florentine girl of the past. When he first sees her veiled figure he cries out to Virgil: 'The embers burn, Virgil, the embers burn'; and afterwards the Virtues of this certainly new life assure him (as if he needed it—the assurance is for us): 'These are the eyes from which Love began to shoot his arrows at you'. And she herself, in a terrible voice, utters the same assurance in the line which has been considered the greatest in all European poetry: 'Look well; we are, we are indeed Beatrice'. She is justified in it by her office, her nature, and her passion; she knows her part in him and has accepted it by her care for his salvation; she knows his duty to her and has accepted that. It is a woman who speaks; it is her last touch of mortality before the heavenly smile breaks through. She comes then, the same Beatrice, in what is called by the commentators 'the Pageant of the Church', and so it is, but it is also the pageant of Beatrice. It halts, and she speaks to him, accusing him—of what? One is not quite clear; Dante did not, in so many words, state it. It is something to do with his genius, of which she frankly reminds him; and something to do with a falsity 'to her buried flesh'. But the Church itself has not insisted that a man should be faithful after her death to a woman whom he loved but had not married. Was the falsity then in some lechery? some tearing by the Panther whom he had never noosed? Or was there something more? some apostacy to the vision? If he had at some moment denied *that*, if he had apostatized from his particular Dantean vocation, if he had been not only 'wanderingly lewd' but foolishly wise, and in some state of despair or other abandonment had denied the validity of Beatrice, then the bitter oration would be entirely justified. However this may be, it is to be noticed that it is still the vision in flesh which is in question. It is to 'mia carne sepulta', 'my buried *flesh*', that Beatrice demands fidelity, the flesh of the girl loved in Florence. It is infidelity to this which, when all lesser sins have been purged, demands a final purging.

It is after this, when even this has been bathed away in Lethe, that the great theological affirmation of the nature of Beatrice takes place. She gazes into the eyes of the Gryphon who is Christ, and It back into hers. There it is mirrored now as one, now as the other, 'immutable in itself, mutable in its image'. The Godhead and the Manhood are, as it were, deeply seen in those eyes whence Love began to shoot its arrows at Dante, by the Glory and the femininity. The moment in the New Life when the girl was seen as the vehicle of Love, preceded by Joan as Christ was preceded by John, is here multiplied and prolonged—one might say, infinitely. The supernatural validity of that 'falling-in-love' experi-ence is again asserted, with every circumstance of accurate definition. In the full Earthly Paradise, she is seen mirroring the Incarnate Splen-dour, as in Florence its light had been about her. 'Look at him,' her attendants entreat her; 'unveil your face that he may see your second beauty.' She does—and he does.

If indeed Dante had at any time denied his proper doctrine of grace, here he renewed and re-asserted it. He was now, in the poem which he had imagined her as helping to create, doing what he had wished and writing of her 'what had not heretofore been written of any woman'. It has become a great classic of literature. But the question this paper is concerned to ask is not so much poetic as realistic; was Dante merely accurate? When young men and young women fall in love, is it true that they do often see each other in an unusual beauty and glory? and if so, was Dante's justification of it itself justified? I will return again to that question at the end.

It is perhaps worth while pausing here to note that, soon after this wonder of revelation, Dante permits himself a moment of celestial laughter. He is shown a vision of the Church in apostacy, and he is moving onward with Beatrice and Matilda, who had drawn him through Lethe, when he asks a question to which he has already been told the answer. Beatrice refers him to Matilda. Matilda protests that she did really explain to him, and Beatrice with a heavenly delight answers: 'Well, yes—perhaps he *has* had other things to think of since then!' She almost says, what she does say presently, 'Lamb!'

The process through Paradise begins. We are in the place of those adult in love; anyone who prefers the *Hell* may be left to the rebuke which Dante imagines Virgil addressing to him when he displayed overmuch interest in hell: 'Once more—and I shall be indignant.' The general idea that the *Hell* is more interesting is true—for those who do not wish to be 'adult in love'. Dante did. The poetic problems are, no doubt, greater; it is almost a measure of Dante's genius that he overcame them as he did. He so overcame them that the reader becomes gradually aware that the interest of all the rest of his work is heightened by this; say, depends on this. Without the *Paradise*, all the rest would be great and moving; with the *Paradise*, though it remains great and moving, it yet dwindles by comparison. The first meetings with Beatrice, thrilling as they are, become less urgent in this world where 'in caritate e qui necesse', love is fate. When she speaks, here, of the 'courage' of Dante's eyes, she is speaking seriously. This is the poetry of experience, and not of theory: the experience of the 'in-Godding' of the self, the taking of the self into God.

This is the purpose and problem of the *Paradise*: how is man in-Godded? the problem to which Beatrice is to lead him to the answer. 'From the first day when I beheld her face in this life until the present moment', Dante says, just before the full revelation of the celestial Rose, my song never ceased to study her.' It is her eyes which his, throughout, study. But what then now are those eyes? and what is the method of the in-Godding which they behold? The whole of the *Paradise* is, as might be expected, greatly beyond our common knowledge. Not until many more lovers have set themselves to follow that Way will it become known and (as far as it ever can) common. The method is the following of the sanctity which is known and understood in romantic love and to which that love was meant to lead. The eyes of Beatrice are still to Dante the direction of the soul knowing sanctity, which is the courtesy of our Lord God, as they had already been to him the vision of the courtesy. In the first canto Dante, bidden to look at the sun, sees as it were a second sun, as if he came into a new universe which was yet the same, 'a new heaven and a new earth'. The earth is certainly there; the body is there; Dante does not forget that vehicle by which all illumination of that Way came. In the fourth circle of heaven, where the great doctors and sages are, Solomon proclaims the doctrine: 'When the glorious and holy flesh shall be reclothed upon us, our persons shall be more acceptable by being more complete . . . the glow we now wear shall be less than the flesh . . . the organs of the body shall be strong to all that can give delight'; and all the circle, desiring their bodies, say *Amen*. This statement is made in answer to Beatrice inquiring on Dante's behalf. It is her business and privilege in the *Paradise* to supply, of herself, or from others, the instruction and knowledge he so passionately desires.

The flesh and the soul are one: that is the nature of the experience of beatitude. The first great maxim of beatitude is announced by the spirit of Piccarda in the first heaven: 'here love is fate'. Dante has asked her whether she and those with her do not grudge the greater glory of others in more advanced Orders of heaven, and she answers, in effect, that such a question is meaningless: 'the quality of love makes quiet the will; if we desired anything other than we have, we should be a discord from his will; to be *thus* is what we most desire; his will is our peace.' We love—what more? This love, each for all, has everywhere due proportion and intensity. Knowledge increases. In the heaven of Venus, beyond which the last shadow of earth does not reach, where the great lovers are, Dante sees Folco of Marseilles (a troubadour and afterwards a Cistercian), to whom he uses the great phrase: 's' io m' intuassi, come tu t' immii', 'if I in-thee'd myself, as thou dost in-me thyself'. In the vision of the Eagle of just kings, he sees that the Eagle *thinks* 'We' and 'Our', but it *says* 'I' and 'mine'. Partnership has become a more intense unity. All this, with other incidents, leads on to the eventual knowing, in a flash, of the last great riddle when he sees the circle which is Christ painted with the image of man: 'I longed to know how the image consorts with the circle, and how it settles there'. He had been given and he had repeated other answers; this, as far as he knew, he could not repeat. But it is the in-Godding of man that he sees.

It is along this way of experienced life that Beatrice accompanies her lover. In the *New Life* no-one had known what she willed; here it is clear—she wills to be for Dante what Dante needs. She has not to write the *Comedy*; she has two points—God and Dante. She lives, of course, like her lover, in and through the great Rose of blessed souls; she is in no sense confined to Dante. But whatever Dante's need requires her to be, that, subject to God, she becomes. 'No-one in the world ever moved so quickly' as she to help him in the beginning, so she told Virgil; and it is perhaps this to which Dante alludes when, in his last cry to her, he says 'O donna, in cui la mia speranza vige'—'O Lady, in whom my *hope* hath vigour . . . preserve thy magnificence in me'. It is beyond even this, after she has turned her eyes for the last time from him to God (so differently from that turning away of the eyes in the refused salutation in Florence), that Bernard, invoking the Blessed Virgin for Dante, says: 'Look how Beatrice, with how many of the blessed, clasp their hands to you'. This is the last vision of her, imploring Deity through the maid-mother that Dante may be there, putting herself still at his disposal. 'O Beatrice, dear and tender guide!'

But she also has been known. There are two great poetic moments in this movement of the two of them along the heavenly way which a little stand out. The first is when she is forgotten; the second is when she is seen. At the opening of the heaven of the doctors she exclaims to him: 'Ringrazia, ringrazia . . .' 'give thanks, give thanks to the Sun of the Angels'. Dante is so moved by devotion at these words, and by desire for God, that for the first time in the whole history he forgets Beatrice altogether. 'Ma si se ne rise—' she is so delighted at this that she laughs at the heavenly infidelity, and 'the splendour of her laughing eyes' catches his mind back from the vision (for which he is not yet ready)—to her? no, but to the glowing lights about him which are the great doctors of the Church. Even in the *Paradise* itself there are few more complex and intense poetic moments—and not many nearer an accurate image of actual experience. This too is a statement of what happens to the most ordinary people in love. A sudden apprehension of the Good takes place, and the very appearance of the admired form is at once forgotten in that and yet excites the mind to ardours of intellect. Such experiences may be brief but they are normal; they are the answer to the everlasting question whether Beatrice is Theology. She is, of course, Theology, but she is only Theology because she is Beatrice; unwomaned, she is also untheologized. 'The glorious and holy flesh' is, in some sense, the exhibition of Theology incarnate; as, because of the Incarnation, it is and must be. And when all these mysteries are hinted, yet in Paradise they can be for awhile happily ignored; the joyous laughter of the Florentine at finding herself at last forgotten is as simple and natural as the surroundings are complex and supernatural. It is precisely a girl laughing in the City whom we hear.

The knowledge of the in-Godding proceeds. In the 23rd canto Dante sees his first glance of Christ triumphing among the redeemed—'one sun which set all burning'. It is then that Beatrice calls to him to look at her indeed—in a voice different from that other invitation of the Earthly Paradise: 'Open thine eyes; look at what I am'—'riguarda'. It is the cry uttered so often through the poem—'look, look well'; and he turns at it now, as she offers herself to his gaze—an offer worthy 'di tanto grado', of 'so great gratitude'. This is the opposite of the false Thais flattery; infinite gratitude here is serious. He sees 'the sacred countenance made clear by the sacred smile', the smile of one of the elect to another, but also the smile of Beatrice for Dante. It is, no doubt, a state of being far beyond the normal, and yet it is but the normal made infinitely profound: many young lovers must have known precisely 'the sacred countenance made clear by the sacred smile'. One can see it happening almost anywhere, in streets, at stations, in drawing-rooms; and even the protest of Beatrice which immediately follows is not alien. She who delights in being studied, whose great profit was to be studied, who carried so much love 'within her sacred eyes', exclaims against it; she turns his attention elsewhere—'why does this face of mine so enamour you that you do not . . .' and so on; and she uses the word 'enamour', '*in*-love', 'innamora'. It is fitting that when, immediately afterwards, Dante is questioned by St. John, the apostle of love, he speaks of her again in the old manner; his own eyes, he says, 'were the gates where she entered with the fire in which I burn for ever'.

It is impossible here to trace the diagram of the final movement. In the heaven which is pure light—'intellectual light full of love'—he sees her at the last point of his power of speech of her; afterwards, directed by St. Bernard, he sees her in her place among the redeemed; he invokes her still to preserve him; they exchange their gaze. There follows the profound and mystical final substitution. The eyes of Beatrice have been the sign and means of ascent in experience; they have shown themselves to Dante and in a sense known heaven for Dante. But at the moment when 'Beatrice and all the blessed' implore the Divine Mother for him, it is not her eyes that the poem names, though it may be her eyes also that the poem means. It is Mary's—'those eyes, loved and venerated by God'. It is the mortal maternity of Godhead that is here expressed. But this also is not alien from the Way: what else had Beatrice seemed when she came after Joan in the mortal city?

'Look well.' The whole poem is composed of variations on that *attention*. But I said at the beginning that the question here is whether this pattern, which is certainly a part of Dante's work, is a pattern to us; whether the diagram of romantic love which it presents, with every circumstance of tenderness and terror, is a diagram of value to us. People are still, it seems, 'falling in love', and a great many of them are falling in love after that manner, or so it still seems. It does not follow that they express it properly, or can so express it. The 'falling in love' may be of many kinds and many degrees; there may be more or less of vision, more or less of affection, more or less of appetite. None of these excludes another. I have already expressed my own belief that the vision is far more common than we who forget or betray or deny it understand. On the other hand, if this is so and if Dante is right, then if we neglect it, we shall neglect, both for ourselves and for others, a Way of Sanctity. Marriage might be the most common exposition of the Way; as, no doubt, in many unknown homes it is. And if so high a potentiality lies in so many lovers' meetings, then those lovers might well be encouraged to believe in the Way and to become aware of what potentialities they hold. It is not to make us heavy and solemn; Eros need not for ever be on his knees to Agape; he has a right to his delights; they are a part of the Way. The division is not between the Eros of the flesh and the Agape of the soul; it is between the moment of love which sinks into hell and the moment which rises to the in-Godding. Beatrice will, no doubt, 'die'. But the eyes from which Love shot his earlier arrows, the eyes which (St. John tells Dante) have the power to clear his blindness, the eyes which are in heaven so full of love for him, the eyes in which the two-natured Gryphon of Christ is reflected, the eyes of the Florentine girl—there are the eyes which in the end change only into the eyes of the Mother of God. This is the unique and lasting mystery of the Way.

111

Principal Works of Charles Williams

1912   *The Silver Stair.* Herbert & Daniel. (verse)
1917   *Poems of Conformity.* Oxford University Press. (verse)
1920   *Divorce.* Oxford University Press. (verse)
1925   *Windows of Night.* Oxford University Press. (verse)
1929   *A Myth of Shakespeare.* Oxford University Press. (verse drama)
1930   *Heroes and Kings.* Sylvan Press. (verse)
　　　 War in Heaven. Victor Gollancz. (novel)
1931   *Many Dimensions.* Victor Gollancz. (novel)
　　　 The Place of the Lion. Mundanus (Victor Gollancz). (novel)
　　　 Three Plays. Oxford University Press. (verse drama)
1932   *The English Poetic Mind.* Clarendon Press. (criticism)
　　　 The Greater Trumps. Victor Gollancz. (novel)
1933   *Bacon.* Arthur Barker. (biography)
　　　 Reason and Beauty in the Poetic Mind. Clarendon Press. (criticism)
　　　 Shadows of Ecstasy. Victor Gollancz. (novel)
1934   *James I.* Arthur Barker. (biography)
1935   *The New Book of English Verse.* Victor Gollancz. (anthology)
　　　 Rochester. Arthur Barker. (biography)
1936   *Queen Elizabeth.* Duckworth. (biography)
　　　 Thomas Cranmer of Canterbury. Oxford University Press. (verse drama)
1937   *Descent into Hell.* Faber & Faber. (novel)
　　　 Henry VII. Arthur Barker. (biography)
　　　 Stories of Great Names. Oxford University Press. (biography)

1938   *He Came Down from Heaven.* Heinemann. (theology)
        Taliessin through Logres. Oxford University Press. (verse)

1939   *Judgement at Chelmsford.* Oxford University Press. (verse drama)
        The Descent of the Dove. Longmans. (theology)

1941   *Witchcraft.* Faber & Faber. (theology)
        Religion and Love in Dante. Dacre Press. (romantic theology)

1942   *The Forgiveness of Sins.* Bles. (theology)

1943   *The Figure of Beatrice.* Faber & Faber. (criticism)

1944   *The Region of the Summer Stars.* Poetry (London) Editions. (verse)

1945   *All Hallows' Eve.* Faber & Faber. (novel)
        The House of the Octopus. Edinburgh House Press. (verse drama)

1946   *Flecker of Dean Close.* Canterbury Press. (biography)

1948   *Arthurian Torso* (containing the first five chapters of the unfinished *The Figure of Arthur*). Oxford University Press. (literary history)

1958   *The Image of the City and Other Essays.* Edited and introduced by Anne Ridler. Oxford University Press. (critical and theological essays)

1963   *Collected Plays.* Edited by John Heath-Stubbs. Oxford University Press. (*Thomas Cranmer of Canterbury, Judgement at Chelmsford, Seed of Adam, The Death of Good Fortune, The House by the Stable, Grab and Grace, The House of the Octopus, Terror of Light, The Three Temptations*)

For details of Williams's reviews and articles, see the Bibliography in Mary McDermott Shideler's *The Theology of Romantic Love: A Study in the Writings of Charles Williams* (Eerdmans, 1962) and Lois Glenn's *Charles W. S. Williams: A Checklist* (Kent State University Press, 1975).

Printed in the United States
65868LVS00006B/128

9 780976 402589